Celebration!

A Woman´s Story of Courage, Endurance, and Transcendence

By
Peggy S. Grose

Some names have been changed for the sake of privacy.

Cover art by Cathy Munson, Austin, Texas

Book design by Jim Brothers

ISBN 0-9744213-2-4

DEDICATION

This story is dedicated to women everywhere, young and old. It is my own journey of self-discovery. It is not about blame but about my own part in creating the quality of my relationships and how I experienced them.

This book is written:
♀ for the woman who is living someone else's goals, either their goals for her or for themselves through her;
♀ for the woman who is looking outside herself for self-esteem and approval;
♀ for the older woman who is stuck in an unfulfilling job or relationship and is hurting but doesn't know why;
♀ for the young woman whose body has not been respected by others so that she has not learned to respect it herself;
♀ to the woman who has not developed a clear idea of who she is;
♀ to the woman who wears a coat of shame and guilt for not being perfect and for not being able to do it all;
♀ to the woman who sees herself as an extension of someone else and doesn't understand why she's hurting;
♀ and to the woman who is dependent and cautious, afraid to speak up and say "no," afraid to reach out and take the risk of asking for what she wants and needs.

May the women who read this book realize their own value, cherish who they are, and know their own worth, and that it is based upon who they are and not upon what others need them for.

May they learn to appreciate and gain from their experiences, value their failures and losses, and transcend it all, reaping the rewards of greater confidence, wisdom, and satisfaction.

ACKNOWLEDGMENTS

Everyone I have ever known or met has, in some way, contributed to my life; and I owe them a great deal. I acknowledge and thank the following people:

- my parents, Thurmon and Willa Smith, who gave me strong genes, good health, and worthwhile values;
- folks in my hometown church, who, as I was growing up, taught me the concept of a loving God and gave me unreserved love and confidence in myself;
- my pastors, Vernard Robertson and Shannon Holloway, who kept a watchful and caring eye on me and pushed me to be all that I could be;
- the extended family on both my mother's and father's side that, during my childhood, were ever so loving and interested in my activities and welfare;
- teachers in elementary school, high school, and college who stretched my mind, challenged me to spread my wings, and had high expectations of me;
- college friends and dorm mates, especially those who were substitute sisters and with whom I could be my outrageous self and still be loved;
- my circle of women friends in Austin who cheer me on;
- my women friends in the Austin Zona Rosa writing group, for their enthusiastic support and feedback on the book;
- friends in the Al-Anon group, with whom I can be honest and from whom I receive unconditional support,
- Jane Barnholdt, Mary Boone, Mavis Bradsher, Claudia Corum, Claudia Snowden, my brother Gene and sister-in-law Brenda, , Faye Steger, Teddy Broeker, Jane Ross, Larry Houser, M.D., Jane Ross, my husband Jim Kilpatrick, and Marty Walker all who lovingly read and commented on the manuscript;
- and my editor and friend, Pat Saunders, who has taught me much about style and formatting while editing the material.

Peggy S. Grose

CONTENTS

PREFACE

by Bob Setty, PhD.

The first time I met Peggy Grose, she was applying for a job as a group therapist and I was doing the hiring. In spite of having fewer academic credentials than the many Ph.D. applicants, Peggy stood out. She clearly had the "right stuff" for the job, possessing the ability to communicate, connect, and inspire our court-referred clients.

When I was interviewing Peggy, it was important to me to hire therapists who had fully experienced life. I recall thinking, *This gal has been around the block.* In fact, from Havana to Singapore to Columbia to Kerrville, Texas, Peggy has been around the world. As long and amazing as her journey across the planet has been, the breadth and length of this outer journey pales in comparison to her inner journey, as detailed in this honest, sometimes humorous, and always unsentimental autobiography, *Celebration!*.

Over several years, I observed Peggy successfully functioning as a change agent with addicts, felons, prostitutes, and bad-check writers. Anyone open to being helped was assisted by her. Clients both respected and liked her as they responded to her caring, respectful attitude and the wealth of information she shared with them.

Peggy was raised to live someone else's life. From the culture of the Deep South in the mid-twentieth century, to her mother's critical voice, to her minister husband's emotional abuse and neglect, Peggy was put on a path to be subservient and secondary, a cheerleader for others. The message to her was "nurture and care for your husband but expect no appreciation; you are not important."

Fortunately, Peggy was just too irrepressible and feisty to abandon herself. Aided by the strong and deep family roots and support from church folk, teachers and friends, Peggy always displayed a capacity to learn from her experiences. She grew throughout her life. As shown in *Celebration!*, Peggy is an active observer; and from an early age, she identified and integrated the lessons that life was teaching her. Through joy and pain, Peggy learned from it all and continued to express her zest for life, no matter how challenging the circumstances.

Throughout her life, Peggy has been a "seeker." Zen Buddhism states that "only seekers get it, but you don't get it by seeking." Peace is not something you acquire; it is achieved after you have laid the right foundation from years of living, of seeking.

Celebration! details Peggy's journey to acceptance and peace. It is a story as honest and real as life itself, reflecting both insight into her own experience and into the human condition in general. *Celebration!* is a powerful memoir, especially for women seeking to find their voices, identity, and esteem in a culture that often does not support them. *Celebration!* is also a universal tale, detailing the power of the human spirit to rise above adversity to a life characterized by fortitude, acceptance, and peace.

After we no longer worked together, Peggy and I stayed in touch. She is a naturally therapeutic individual in the best sense of the word. Lunch with Peggy, always honest and unpretentious, would inevitably leave me feeling better about myself and life after the thought-provoking conversation that would inevitably arise. It has been enriching for me to know Peggy and the story of her life. With *Celebration!*, Peggy has shared her story, one that will be a true gift for all who read it.

INTRODUCTION

Ernie, a long-time friend and co-worker, left his job in order to start a private, nonprofit, outpatient, drug treatment program and asked me to join him. I was delighted to be part of this creative venture and to be working again with my buddy. Now we could build a program from the ground up, with none of the toxic elements of so many work places, and I had carte blanche to create a model program. Using a state-of-the-art style of counseling, I would use my experience in writing curriculum for chemical dependency programs, in counseling, and in directing such programs.

I wrote the first six sessions for beginning clients while still laid up after foot surgery and began conducting group counseling sessions as soon as I could get around. I was still on crutches when I completed a client workbook of 18 sessions at home, with extra notes and instructions for a facilitator.

I bought floral arrangements at a garage sale for the waiting room, shelves for the storage closets and art prints for the meeting rooms and painted the poster frames to match the upholstered chairs.

Ernie started paying me as soon as he had some money coming in, but I still put in many hours that did not go on my timesheet. It was my choice, for I was having a wonderful time creating something exceptional.

A gifted student sought us out because of the style of program I was implementing and became my intern. One evening after an especially powerful group session, Harry observed, "Peggy, this is textbook!" This was significant because, while most Licensed Chemical Dependency Counselors are well versed in the area of chemical dependency education, few have had much training or experience in the counseling process itself or in facilitating groups. We were becoming recognized as a model program in the community. Our group sessions "rocked," and I felt greatly rewarded.

Ernie became hostile and emotionally and verbally abusive after about a year. Talking with him accomplished little, much to my frustration, as I watched our friendship and working relationship crumble. It began to feel very old, like something I recognized all too well from past experiences.

At the end of two years, Ernie called me at home the day after Christmas and asked me to come to the office. I had felt something ominous brewing in the previous few weeks and, because his voice was shaking that morning, I knew what was about to happen. I said to my husband as I left the house, "I'm about to be canned," and to myself I said, *Be like a rock.*

Ernie began by informing me that I had become more of a liability than an asset and went on to enumerate my shortcomings. At the end he asked, "How do you feel about this?"

"Oh, Ernie," I replied, "I'm so relieved. It's been so long since I have felt safe with you." He was obviously taken aback. I completed the month, said goodbyes to my beloved clients, and left graciously.

The irony of all this is that I had been miserable for a year and would have left sooner, but I thought Ernie and the program couldn't get along without me. Now I had to examine closely the pattern of my whole life; this situation seemed all too familiar. It was a repeat of my old pattern of over-investing, overdoing and, in the absence of appreciation, trying harder.

That's when I began to write my story. It's about my adventures into unknown places, both into the outside world and into my inner world. It's about my journey and how I experienced it. One might say that, by writing this book, I am trying to make sense of my life. At age 75, I have finally learned the lessons that life has been trying to teach me all along.

This book also is about courage—the courage to venture into the unknown, outside one's comfort zone. For me, that meant

Celebration!

going into new places, meeting new people, and expanding my world. It took courage to go to foreign lands, to face the fear, but even more courage to venture inside myself. Yet, I have discovered that most of the "goodies" in life are outside that comfort zone.

The process has truly been healing and enlightening, and I trust it will be so for you. I sought inner guidance as I wrote these pages, with the hope that the words will be healing and not hurtful.

Please be kind to my story and to the characters in it. I trust that your reading will be as much a blessing as writing it has been for me.

FOREWORD

SNAKES IN THE OUTHOUSE

We moved to a run-down farm just before the start of World War II, when I was eight. The dilapidated house sat close to the railroad tracks and had no electricity or running water, so we had no indoor plumbing. We couldn't get lines brought over to provide electricity because of wartime shortages and were without these conveniences until after the conflict ended.

We did have a few snakes, however, and I was terribly afraid of them, especially in the yard after dark. I vividly remember at least one occasion when I, the only girl in the family, needed to go to the outhouse but had no one to accompany me. Maybe Mama was sick, or maybe she was away taking care of some sick relative, as she often did. No matter.

I was afraid there would be snakes along the path or in the outhouse itself. I dreaded it but had to go. I took a boxful of matches, striking them to brighten the way as I inched along the path. I stood at the door, striking matches and looking into all the corners to make sure nothing sinister was waiting for me.

Guess what? Never once did I encounter any snakes, on the path or in the outhouse. I did learn from the experience this important thing, however: Courage is not the absence of fear; it's doing the thing one must do in the face of fear, all the while knowing what could be waiting.

I realized that I wasn't afraid of snakes in the daytime, that there were no more snakes in the darkness than there were in the light, and that it was what I couldn't see that frightened me. On the other hand, just because I couldn't see a thing didn't mean it wasn't there.

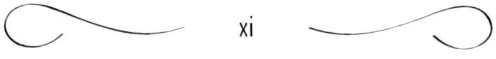

Celebration!

This was one of the earliest and most important experiences of my life. It taught me to go with the fear and not let it hold me back.

> **Take the risk of doing the thing you would do
> if you were not afraid.**

CHAPTER ONE

EARLY CHILDHOOD

I was born in the "Uncle Claude house," a piece of property that was part of the original land grant made to my great, great, great, great, great-grandfather for having served in the Revolutionary War. My great-uncle had owned this farm and lived there during his lifetime, and now my parents were renting and farming the land.

I made my entrance early in the morning on August 24, 1933, on a farm near Bellville, Georgia. Franklin Delano Roosevelt was president, and John Nance Garner was vice president. Charles Laughton, playing in *The Private Life of Henry VIII*, was voted best actor, and Katherine Hepburn, best actress in *Morning Glory*. Bread was 7 cents a loaf; milk, 41 cents a gallon; gas, 18 cents a gallon; stamps, 3 cents each; and a car cost $550.

I've been told that when it seemed that I was ready to enter this world, Daddy walked down the lane to his parents' house, the house in which he was born, to telephone Dr. Wallace Daniel to come. Dr. Daniel had been the family physician for several generations and was a close friend of my grandparents. When he arrived, I was still not quite ready to make my appearance, so he left to check on some other patients in the area. When he returned, since I was still not in sight, the doctor ate a breakfast of eggs, grits, ham, and sausage and then lay down for a nap.

After I was delivered, the doctor came out of the room and teased Daddy. "Well, Thurmon, you have another little boy," he announced.

"Oh, no, not another nasty little boy!" my paternal grandmother groaned.

Celebration!

When Daddy came back out of the room, he chided, "Doc, you'd better go back and take another look!"

They say my daddy doted on me when I was a tyke, but I don't remember anything about that. I do remember that he often carried me on his back with my feet in the back pockets of his overalls. When he abandoned the overalls for regular pants, I was disappointed that I couldn't ride anymore because it would pull his pants off.

Until my father's time, almost everyone in the community called "Smith Town"-the original land grant- was related and parcels had been handed down through the generations. During Daddy's lifetime, the descendents began to sell off their parcels so that the only Smiths living in the community today are my cousins, Walter and William Smith and their families.

I've learned recently that my grandfather, Commodore Beecher Smith, was named after the famous minister and anti-slavery activist, Henry Ward Beecher. Henry was the brother of Harriet Beecher Stowe, the author of *Uncle Tom's Cabin.* Granddaddy Beecher was a much-respected member of the community. He spearheaded a plan to set up a school in the area so that children who had to walk could easily attend, and he held weekly prayer meetings at his house. He was known for his respectfulness toward "colored" people.

I remember a few of Daddy's uncles and aunts, some of whom still lived in the area when I was growing up, although they were pretty old by then. I knew just about all of Grandmama Smith's siblings because she was younger than Granddaddy.

That fifth great-grandfather and many family members from subsequent generations are buried in The Simon-Smith cemetery just down the road from the "Home Place." That's what we call the last parcel still in the family after 200 years and where Daddy was born and died. He bought the farm in 1961 from his brother Hoke, who had owned it after my grandmother died. That's where I took my boys many summers as they were growing up. The boys appreciate knowing their Smith roots, having known none of their dad's relatives besides his parents.

There is an interesting story about Jim Bell, a half-brother of my Granddaddy Beecher. The wife of Daniel Smith, Jim B.'s father, owned their farm, and when she died, her property went to her sons. Daniel remarried and had a son, Jim B., by his second wife. When Daniel died, the half-brother, having been left out of the first mother's will, received no property, and most of the brothers declined to share theirs. This hurt Jim B. so that he decided to leave for California. My grandfather and his brother Stuart begged him to stay and offered to share their small acreage with him.

I ought to add that Jim B. was accused of some "irregular" transactions at the bank where he worked and would have done some jail time had it not been for the governor, who was a relative. The governor assigned him to work at the governor's mansion, instead, where he served out his time.

Considering all that, Jim B. moved west and changed his name to Stuart Anthony, after his Uncle Stuart and a friend named Anthony. The family never saw or heard from him again but heard about him after he became a screenwriter of some note. We even went to see one of his movies, *The Biscuit Eater.* In later years, Daddy's brother Conrad researched and found Jim B.'s children, who were ecstatic to learn they had family in Georgia and visited their newly discovered relatives.

Daddy's brothers were a fascinating lot. The oldest was Conrad, followed by Daddy, and then his brothers Hoke, Clarence, and C.B. Sisters Nell and Mildred came between Clarence and C.B.

Conrad was an agnostic and sworn socialist. Articulate, widely read, and with a keen mind, he spoke with eloquence about the sorry state of the government, the lack of brotherhood in the world, and the disgraceful way the government treated its veterans. With a great shock of black hair and a huge, black mustache, he made up with fiery oratory for his lack of stature. I remember relatives muttering under their breath, "Conrad's a communist!" But he was fun and one of my favorite uncles. When he saw me, he would say, "Hey, Beautiful, when are you going to Hollywood?"

No wonder I liked him, huh?

Conrad was an amateur magician with a superb sense of humor and always entertained us with tricks, stories, and jokes. He was good enough to be professional, and it was he who inspired and mentored my brother Gene's son, Sammy, who is a now a professional magician. Conrad was murdered in his home at age 80 by an intruder who left Conrad's pockets turned wrong side out.

It was hard to take, especially for Gene and Sammy.

On the other extreme were Hoke, the third-born, and C.B., the youngest. They were both ultraconservative fundamentalists and tried to get all the rest of us "saved." They were certain that we Methodists would burn in hell if they didn't do something about it.

C.B., now the only survivor of the seven siblings, has been a career evangelist and, while I never agreed with his style or his theology, I must say that he still has a great memory for reciting scripture and a wonderful command of the English language. Though he is not highly educated, he can pray the most eloquent prayers I have ever heard. He constantly talks "pig Latin" and is as corny as "Kansas in August."

We can't help but laugh.

Daddy was next in line after Conrad and the only one that followed farming as his life's work. He was short in stature but a hard worker. A story that he told me more than once, weeping, was of the day when he picked more cotton than his brother Hoke, and for that, Granddaddy gave the younger boy a whipping. I have a hunch that that is the reason Daddy could never say "no" to Hoke, who often took advantage of him.

And maybe that's the reason Mama, who got little cooperation from Daddy, so resented Hoke.

Next was Clarence, who was bright, well educated, and hand-some in his Navy uniform during the war. Before joining the Navy, Clarence taught school at Richmond Hill, Georgia, a small community near Savannah, most of which was owned by Henry Ford. Clarence wrote to Ford about the disrepair of the school and the need for many improvements. Ford rode up in his big car a few days later with a check for building a brand new school, complete with the necessary supplies and equipment and musical instruments for a band. He and Clarence became good friends.

Clarence worked as a chemist at a paper mill after the war and at an Owens-Illinois pulpwood plant in Orange, Texas. He later retired and moved to Florida to work for my brother Gene, who looked after him like a son when "C.L." grew old and senile.

Daddy's sisters Nell and Mildred were both quite normal, with happy marriages and well-adjusted children.

Mama's siblings were good, solid people, though not as color-ful as Daddy's. Matsy was one year older than Mama, then came Elizabeth, whom they called "Tiny" because of her size, then Jack, Neal, Mary, and Janet.

Matsy taught school for nearly 40 years. She was married to William Deal, whom Mama's family called "Deal" instead of "William." Matsy was prim and proper, always in a happy mood, with perfect manners. They never had children. Uncle Deal was a temperamental musician who could blow up without warn-ing. They lived in the same city where I went to college, and I was in their home often. My roommate Patty and I occasionally hiked the three miles to their house on the edge of town.

One Sunday, the table was beautifully set with bone china, crystal, linen napkins and table cloth, and sterling silverware when Patty and I had dinner with them. Aunt Matsy said some-thing that set Uncle Deal off and he became belligerent.

"Darling!" Aunt Matsy exclaimed, with a look of surprised alarm.

Celebration!

Uncle Deal slammed his napkin into his plate and declared, "I'm going to the woods!" and stormed out.

I know that Matsy was mortified, but she said nothing and carried on as if nothing had happened. I was embarrassed for her. Yet, they were a devoted couple, openly affectionate and demonstrative with each other.

Mama was one year younger than Matsy and always a farm wife. Elizabeth, the mother of my cousins Barbara, Dick and Marilyn, was an assistant manager at Grant's Department Store for her whole career and could have been the manager if she had been willing to transfer to another city. She had been divorced for many years. Mary worked at various jobs, the last of which was with a City of Savannah agency. Jack owned a dry cleaners, and Neal worked his whole career with Southern Bell Telephone. Janet taught school after raising her one daughter and, except for Mama and Matsy, they all lived in Savannah for most of their adulthood.

Uncle Neal, my cousin Eleanor's dad, was the only person I knew that smoked cigars, and I liked the scent. If I came home from school and smelled cigar smoke in the house, I was delighted to know my Uncle Neal was there.

Granny Rushing was a straight-laced, upright woman who always appeared busy and businesslike. She ran a small "confectionary" store on the corner of Victory Drive and Jefferson Streets, within walking distance of their home in Savannah. Uncle Jack's cleaners and laundry occupied the back part of the building. Granny was so honest that during the war, when candy was rationed, she refused to let family members have more than their allotment from her store.

Grandpa Rushing was known throughout the state as a brilliant and handsome man. My brother Gene tells of being stopped on the street in our town by Dr. Griffin, who had been in medical school with our grandpa.

He asked, "Aren't you Dolfus Rushing's grandson?"

"Yesser," Gene replied.

"I want you to know that he was one of the smartest people I ever knew," Dr. Griffin declared.

Grandpa did not live up to his potential, but squandered his gifts. We were told that, as a child, he was pampered by his older sisters. He dropped out of medical school after two years because he couldn't tolerate the sight of blood and became a school teacher. Sometimes he taught school, occasionally was the principal, the superintendent at other times, and the family moved often.

He was a philanderer, along with his brilliance and good looks. There is a story of a time when he came home with a bullet hole in his hat, put there by the husband of one of his lady friends. Aunt Mary told me about the time that she accompanied her mother to a woman's house where she confronted Grandpa.

A smoker, he was chronically ill with asthma as long as I can remember. It caused such severe coughing and wheezing that he injected himself with morphine every few hours to get relief. I don't remember him any other way. The shots were so regular that there were times when he had to search his body for flesh that would accommodate the needle. I watched as he heated water in a tablespoon over a can of Sterno™, waited for it to cool, and then added the narcotic that he injected.

He owned a farm in "the country" and periodically made a trip to look after his property, stopping at our house for a few days. He slept poorly at night and was up regularly, coughing and wheezing until he could get the medication. Not only did he keep us awake with his coughing and wheezing; he moaned and groaned—loudly—a play for sympathy, no doubt.

I'm afraid we weren't very sympathetic because by morning, as we faced the day, we were exhausted from lack of sleep while he was snoring away. This annoyed Daddy, particularly.

Grandpa drove an old panel truck, a '31 model Chevrolet painted silver that we dubbed "The Silver Meteor" after the passenger train of the same name. It made such a loud noise that one could hear it from half a mile down the highway. One afternoon, I was in the pecan orchard not far from the house when I heard him coming. I ran in to inform Mama, "Grandpa's coming!" and, sure enough, here he came a few minutes later.

The years during the Great Depression were lean and long; and from the stories I have heard, I gather that they left a deep scar on many folks. Daddy scratched out a living by working the soil, and he loved it, though it was a struggle. He told me more than once of a time when corn was bringing 28 cents a bushel— that's 7 cents a peck. There were usually 80 pounds of corn in a bushel, 56 pounds if it was shucked and shelled. But during this particular year, the crop was so sorry that it took more than a bushel to make 80 pounds.

Daddy went into town early one week in August to confer with Floyd Baggett, who ran a grocery store and gristmill and bought farm products. Mr. Floyd promised to pay him 32 cents for his corn, shucked and shelled.

Daddy and Lenny Mincey, his "colored man," worked all week in the field from sunup until to sundown, gathered the corn all day and shucked and shelled it by hand until midnight, until they had 50 bushels of corn. On Saturday, dog-tired, they hitched the two mules to the wagon, loaded the corn, and off they went to market. Daddy was anticipating having a little cash because he needed to bring home some supplies for the family, which included my mother and two brothers. Lenny was looking forward to his pay of 40 cents a day.

When they arrived at Baggett's store, Mr. Floyd informed Daddy that he was so sorry, but that the price had dropped, and he could offer him only 28 cents. Imagine the utter disappointment! Their efforts would bring *4 cents a bushel less* than anticipated.

Daddy had a notion to haul his load back home and feed it to the hogs, but he had almost killed his mules already, hauling those 2,800 pounds over dirt roads in the heat. And besides, he needed whatever cash he could collect. With a heavy heart, he took the $14. He ended his story by adding, "I promised myself that day that I may starve to death in my lifetime, but it sure won't be while shucking and shelling corn!"

Another story he told is of a time after we had moved to that run-down farm I mentioned. He didn't have a penny to plant the next season's crop or to support the family of five. We had an old Chevrolet that he drove to Statesboro, a town nearby, and traded for two mules and a load of hay. Then, back home, he traded the mules to Mr. Aubrey Ollif for the down payment on a one-row tractor and traded the hay for a barrel of gasoline from his good friend Ernest Strickland. It took a barrel a week to run the tractor.

The war began soon after our move, and Daddy sought employment as a carpenter at Camp Stewart, which was being upgraded to Fort Stewart. Having had little experience as a carpenter, he purchased a carpenter's nail apron and scrubbed it around in the dirt to make it look well-used. He constructed a toolbox, collected some old tools, and ventured forth. The superintendent was impressed by the fact that Daddy had a toolbox, which was, to him, an indication that Daddy was eager to work, and he hired him on the spot.

When others began being laid off, he went to the superintendent and explained his financial straits.

The compassionate man advised him to hang around and look busy so that when the hiring began again, he would be first in line.

Daddy went around banging on the barracks with his hammer for several days, pretending to be busy by installing windows in the unfinished hospital and taking them out again. The ruse worked. He was rehired and worked there until the last nail was driven in that army base.

He got his next job at the shipyard in Savannah, where he suffered from the intense heat in the summer and extreme cold in one of the severest winters in memory. "Working on that waterfront, no matter how many pairs of pants I put on, that cold, wet wind went right through them," he remarked, years later. "That was the hardest work a man ever done."

Again, Daddy was retained when others were laid off because he was small and agile and could climb onto high places. He plowed until midnight on his little tractor with its one headlight and then got up again at 5:00 the next morning for the long drive to his day job. He worked at the shipyard until he had saved enough to buy seed to plant crops in the spring.

Daddy went to an agency that offered c-loans, last-resort-financial assistance for families during that time.

"Mr. Smith," the interviewer asked him, "what do you think your weekly run bill would be for your family of five?" A run bill was the cost of things such as groceries, medicine, and school clothes.

"About five dollars," Daddy answered.

"Mr. Smith, you're going to have to lower your standard of living!" the man declared and turned him down. This same man came to him later and apologized, but Daddy said he was glad he hadn't gotten the loan—he didn't want to be beholden to anyone.

My whole family on Daddy's side overdid the Puritan Work Ethic. Daddy's whole life was work. On occasions when we went away as a family to see relatives, on the way home he would say, "My, what I could have gotten done today in this good weather. I could have plowed half the orchard."

The most extreme example, however, is my Aunt Mildred, Daddy's sister. She and her sister Nell lived about 45 miles apart and were together a lot. When Aunt Mildred needed to have a hysterectomy, she arranged to have it done in Baxley where Nell lived, unbeknownst to her husband Uncle Charlie. She didn't want Uncle Charlie to miss a day of work at their laundry. In the evening after the surgery, she called and informed him of her whereabouts and that it was all right for him to come see her. It burned Uncle Charlie up that she hadn't let him know about the surgery and, according to family members, he never quite got over it.

One of my earliest memories is of the day when I was three or four and my parents were at the "home place" for Aunt Nell's wedding. "Aunt Sue," a Black woman who often worked for us, had been left in charge. I suppose my brothers and I got into some sort of mischief, for I remember Aunt Sue chasing us around and around the house with a switch. I don't recall whether she ever caught us or not, but I know my mother was upset with her.

This was the same Aunt Sue who terrified my brother Jack by threatening to put him in the ground if he didn't stop sucking his thumb. There, she said, the Devil would come and get him! If Jack awoke at night and discovered his thumb in his mouth, he would scream, "Don't tell Aunt Sue! Don't tell Aunt Sue!"

My family was so straight-laced that I seldom heard a curse word and certainly never had one come out of my mouth. That included "taking the Lord's name in vain." I may have been three or four when I accompanied Daddy to town the day he ran into his old friend Harry Smith. How delighted they were to see each other.

"Thurmon Smith! Good God A'mighty! It's so good to see you!" Mr. Harry exclaimed as he grabbed Daddy's hand and shook it enthusiastically.

I was greatly impressed with this language. I loved the way those powerful words, "Good God A'mighty!" rolled off his tongue. I tucked them away in my mind until such time as I would need to call them forth. When finally an occasion arose that was worthy of such fine words, I let it roll: "Good God A'mighty!" I exclaimed.

"Where did you hear that?" my stunned parents wanted to know.

"Mr. Harry Smith," I proudly admitted. But it was not well received by my parents, and I never uttered those words again.

I liked "Miss" Mamie Daniels, my first-grade teacher. Mrs. Thomas, who lived across the street from us and taught another grade, picked me up for school each morning, drove me home for lunch, and took me back to school for the afternoon.

Celebration!

When Mrs. Thomas came the first afternoon to take me back to school, I informed her that I didn't plan to return to school for the rest of the day and to please inform "Miss Mamie" that I would "see her tomorrow." My mother and Mrs. Thomas, laughing, assured me that was not the plan, and I went willingly—once I understood what was expected.

The only time I was ever homesick was while visiting my paternal grandmother who lived alone on the family homestead later in life. Daddy wanted me to stay with her some during the summer, which I did occasionally, but I soon became homesick and called him to come get me.

The house was white, with four columns across the porch, four rocking chairs and a swing on each end; and four majestic, 50-year-old oak trees stood guard over the place. Across the road and down the lane was the house where I was born, surrounded by pretty fields with a backdrop of tall pines. There were few cars on the road back then because the road wasn't paved, so it was peaceful.

Grandmama believed in turning in soon after dark in order to save electricity, so we ate an early supper and sat on the front porch to watch the sun set in front of us. As darkness crept in, the frogs in the ditch began to croak, the crickets began to chirp, and I began to imagine what was happening at my house at that moment. Daddy and the boys would be coming in from the field, Mama would have supper ready on the wood stove— yes, even in summer—the kerosene lamps would be glowing, and there would be a lot of hustle and bustle. Tears began to roll down my cheeks, silently; I didn't want Grandmama to notice.

When I awoke the next morning to hear her talking sweetly to the birds on her windowsill, I was content; but come the darkness, I was homesick again. Since those days, I have spent many an hour on that porch. It's my favorite place to sit while relishing the same scene. One evening, my brothers and I watched an electrical storm in the west give a spectacular performance exactly in front of us, as if set upon a stage.

My parents later lived and died there, and I seldom go back.

The oak trees are gone. The beetles ate them from the inside so that they were weakened and easily destroyed when a tornado came.

Perhaps there is a metaphor here: Sometimes we are more concerned with external, material matters than with developing inner strength. Then, when life's storms blow in, we have few inner resources to endure.

The farm is still in the family, and I plan to go soon and sit for a while.

Roots are important.

CHAPTER TWO

LEARNING MY PLACE

I knew intuitively from an early age, that the importance of my existence was to make my mother look good. Of course, I wouldn't have been able to verbalize this, for it did not become a conscious realization until I was an adult. Mama made sure that I acted in ways that she perceived her friends and family would approve of. She put me into "expression" lessons when I was in fourth grade and piano when I was 12. I was in school plays and choir and active in my church, which had a strong youth program.

I often made a talk or led in prayer when the youth group took over the Sunday evening church service, and the preacher sometimes called on me to lead in prayer, impromptu. I received much love and encouragement from my church community, for whom I could do no wrong.

When I was invited to give a reading at the rotary club for their noon meeting, the school principal called me from class and took me with him. Once, I recited *The Night Before Christmas* for a party at the church.

I took very well to all this, being a natural extrovert, and enjoyed the appreciative attention. When I played the piano or organ or made a speech, however, Mama stood at the door and savored all the compliments for herself, but on the way home, reviewed everything I had done wrong. For many years, when I performed or presented before an audience, I heard her voice in my head, sneering, *You?* I silently replied, *Thank you, Mama, for sharing.*

Yet, I appreciate the many special advantages that she worked hard to provide.

She and I gathered pecans every fall in order to buy a piano for me, and I'm sure she scrounged to pay for the lessons. She also taught me values, the importance of proper table manners, correct English and diction, how to set a table properly, and to watch out for boys and not be "forward" toward them. She did not want us to read "funny books" (comics) or listen to "hillbilly" music, which our parents thought were trashy. Oh, I was very well behaved. I would not have dared to be otherwise. It's interesting to observe how others' expectations of us mold our behavior, especially in a large, extended family or in a small town.

Thus, when my seventh-grade teacher, Mrs. Ponder, embarrassed me and hurt my feelings, I was crushed. Of all my teachers, she is the only one who was ever, for one minute, unkind. Being the helpful child that I was, I raised my hand one afternoon and asked permission to erase the board.

"Well, Peggy, is the board bothering you?" she sarcastically asked.

"Yes, ma'am," I answered, not meaning to be impudent in any way.

"Well, then you may go stand in the hall," she ordered.

There I stood outside the room, in tears, my heart broken. Other students passing by inquired about the problem, but I was too humiliated to answer.

My mother shamed me when I told her about it. I had brought disfavor upon myself and thus upon her because, apparently, she thought everything was about her. I never again confided in her, even when I had some sort of obstruction in my colon. Going to the bathroom was extremely painful for a week or two, until one day it passed and I got relief.

At times, in my presence, someone would compliment Mama on her pretty little girl.

"Oh, she's all right, I guess," she would say, looking down at me.

I knew that the comment pleased Mama but understood that the reason for her off-handed response was that she didn't want me to be conceited. I knew that she criticized her sister for telling her daughters they were pretty. And perhaps that is why I came to believe that *looking* good was not as important as *being* good.

Another early memory is of a hot summer day in Southern Georgia when I was six or eight and accompanied Mama to a flower show at the community center in town. It was a low, white, frame building with a cement floor and lazily revolving overhead fans. The beautiful flowers were arranged on rows of tables up and down the big room.

What caught my eye, though, was a punch bowl at the far end; and I started begging, but Mama put me off. "Let's wait until we finish looking at the flowers, then we'll surely have something to drink," she promised. We made our way up and down between the tables, Mama carefully studying each arrangement and making note of who had won the coveted gold, blue, and white ribbons.

Not me. I kept my eye on another prize. My mouth watered just thinking about how cool and sweet the beverage would be.

After what seemed to me a very long trek, we arrived, finally, at the ultimate destination. The woman serving, a Mrs. Brewton, picked up a pretty glass cup, filled it and handed it to my mother. Then, with a meaningful, condescending look at my eager little face, she put down her ladle and folded her hands.

I bore the humiliation in silence, as my mother drank her punch.

On the way home, Mama explained that she realized how disappointed I was, but that she hadn't known what to do in the situation.

I would have given you my punch, I remember thinking, even as young as I was. It was one of my earliest lessons—that I mattered—just not very much.

Mama suffered from varicose veins in her legs, especially after being on her feet all day. They looked ominous, like dark blue worms crawling underneath her skin. She told me how likely it was that they could burst, causing her to bleed to death. I felt frightened for her and frustrated that I didn't know what to do. Surely I was supposed to do something about it.

What happened to my mother in her childhood that so wounded her? I was never been able to learn much about her early life. Whenever I asked her about it, she murmured, "I Don't remember," and whenever I asked her siblings, they didn't remember either. I Don't think it's because they didn't want to tell, but rather because she didn't know much about herself and because they didn't know much about her either.

One of the few stories she told of her childhood more than once is of a time when she was in fourth grade, and her daddy was her teacher. A girl behind Mama whispered her name, "Willa," and, just as Mama turned around, Grandpa looked up. He brought both of the girls to the front of the room and gave them a sound whipping. He wouldn't be accused of favoring his own daughter.

Mama was second oldest of seven children born within ten years. (No wonder Granny found sex disgusting.) She was overshadowed by her sister who was just one year older. Matsy was as brilliant and talented as their father and more outgoing and confident than Mama. Their grandfather recognized Matsy's abilities and musical talent and financed her education at a boarding school while Mama was left at home to help care for the younger siblings. Once grown, Mama had few skills and limited education, even though she was surely quite smart herself. She married Daddy, a poor farmer, and lived in an old, rundown farmhouse while Matsy, a professional woman, married an accomplished musician, had a nice house, and drove a fine car. It's just a conjecture, you understand; I'm no analyst.

Yet, I have much to be thankful for. Not least is the fact that my church and family didn't threaten me with hell from an early age and that, on the contrary, I was always told of a loving God. I'm sure my parents vaguely believed in hell, but as Methodists, we didn't worry or talk about it at all. I was taught tolerance and brotherly love toward those of other races and religions, as well.

Celebration!

My parents were both outgoing, with charming personalities, and welcomed anyone and everyone into our home.

I also recall a happy childhood. I was delighted when girl cousins came from the city during the summer, especially because I had no sisters. I taught them to swim in the fish pond, drive the tractors, shell peas, go carefully barefoot through the sand burrs, and pick peanuts off the vine, snapping the wrist sharply to get the nut off without the stem.

We lay on the diving board to get tanned, applying generous amounts of baby oil and iodine to hasten the process, and tried new hairstyles. Once we bleached our bangs in accord with the latest fad, for which I was severely scolded. My cousins Barbara, Marilyn, and I were headed to the house through the pasture one afternoon after swimming, when we spotted the aggressive bull headed our way. We climbed into a tree and waited for quite a while to be rescued.

Another year, I was teaching Barbara to drive our Jeep, a new purchase after the war was over. We were in a back field, and Barbara was at the wheel, driving along a narrow, dirt road parallel to the fence. The road was bumpy from the terraces Daddy had plowed into the soil to prevent erosion. It was July, and the fence was loaded with Concord grape vines. It seemed to groan under the weight of those fat, green leaves and luscious, purple grapes waiting to be picked.

"Slow down here," I warned Barbara, "the road is rough."

Instead, she pressed the accelerator and, in a panic, swerved and sideswiped the fence, tearing off about six feet of those wonderful grape vines.

Barbara was older than I and was far more sophisticated and daring than I. And more creative. We picked up the damaged vines, at her suggestion, brushed away our tracks with them, and reattached them to the fence to hide the evidence. Daddy commented, a few evenings later at the supper table, "Something strange has happened to the grapevine in that back field; a whole section has died."

Barbara and I glanced at each other but didn't say a word. Years later, when I was too old for a spanking, I confessed.

Cousins Walter, Jerry, and William came to visit occasionally and, at one point, stayed quite a while. They were too young to help with the farming, and I was often delegated to look after them. I put the older one to work in the kitchen; and to this day, Walter recalls how I taught him to wash dishes—the glasses first, then the dishes, and the pots and pans last.

Jerry, the second-oldest, was born with feet that were so garishly twisted and bent back so far to his legs that the doctors gave him no chance of ever walking. His feet were put into casts the day he was born, and he spent much of his young life in a Shriners' Hospital where he had many surgeries and recuperation periods. He was out of the cast but still wearing braces on one visit. Those were deadly weapons, so he could usually have his way.

My cousin Dick came from Savannah to live with us when I was entering my senior year in high school and remained there with my parents until he graduated a year after me. We cousins have happy memories of those days and are all good friends to this day.

Those who lived in the cities had "victory gardens" to supplement what they could buy to eat; but of course we had about 175 acres of garden, so we ate well and shared what we had. The war years were not as hard on us as on many people, for we had plenty of food and did not need stamps. The main hardship was the lack of sugar for our iced tea, and the alternatives— cane syrup and saccharin—were not tasty.

The speed limit was 35 miles per hour, and most folks restricted their driving because of lack of rubber. Once their tires were gone, that was it for the duration of the war. I Don't believe that affected us because we didn't do much driving anyway. We covered the top half of our headlights at night, so that in case of an attack, the enemy pilots could not see where to drop the bombs.

Celebration!

We practiced air raids. Mama and Gene served on the civilian sky watch, an around-the-clock program for spotting enemy planes, which they learned to identify. Powerful spotlights constantly scanned the sky at night. I remember saving toothpaste tubes and "tin foil" so that the metal could be used for manufacturing arms.

Five hundred thousand German prisoners of war were shipped home when the war was over and many of them returned later to live in America.

Lacking indoor plumbing, we had to get water from a well that was built into the porch just outside the kitchen door. It was easy just to step out and draw up a bucket but not a pleasant chore on a frigid morning. We had an icebox that the iceman replenished two or three times a week on his regular rounds. We had a card that we put in the window to indicate how much ice we needed, saving him a trip back to the truck.

I learned to cook standing beside my mother at the old wood stove. Mama was a wonderful cook, throwing all her energy into preparing delicious food. And I learned from her that all it takes to be a good cook is the willingness to put in the effort and a little imagination as well. Her reputation rested upon her scrumptious creations. We had little cash but ate like royalty, with plenty of vegetables fresh from the garden; fruits and nuts from the orchard; beef, pork, chicken, eggs from the barnyard; and fish from the pond. Gene and Jack went "frog gigging" at the pond occasionally and brought the frogs home for Mama to cook the legs—a delicacy—and sometimes Daddy brought in wild game.

Mama spared no effort at putting great food on the table, but she didn't serve it up with loving words. Suppertime was an opportunity for her to berate Daddy for something such as putting up another tobacco barn (as if that's not what farmers do) or me for something such as shaving my legs or bleaching my bangs (as if that's not what teenage girls do). I was a grown woman with children of my own before I realized that providing food was her way of giving love. Without the loving words, however, the gesture went right over our heads.

This realization inspired me to write the book *Love and Lemon Pie, Recipes for the Body and the Soul.* In this book, I share "recipes for the body" that I have collected for 50 years and on which I raised my four sons and "recipes for the soul," suggestions for communicating in loving and nurturing ways. When I promote the book at signings, I explain, "Here are two very important ways of expressing love—food and the loving words with which we serve it up."

As the only girl, my place was in the house helping Mama while my brothers worked in the fields with Daddy. We fed hired hands occasionally, but mostly we cooked for friends and hordes of relatives from the city, especially in the summer. Mama's sisters often came with their children to visit and to can vegetables to take home.

Special occasions in the summer were "peanut boilings." We fixed the nuts for ourselves, usually; but to some people, these were social events, especially out in the county. Early in the morning, we pulled up the green peanut vines in the field, shook the dirt off, and hauled them on a flatbed trailer to a shelter where we parked to get out of the sun. There, we picked the nuts off the vine with a quick twist of the wrist; and at the house, we rinsed and rinsed and rinsed away the sand with water from the well, boiled the peanuts on the kitchen stove, and added salt at the end of an hour. The salt couldn't begin to penetrate the shell until after the pot was taken off the fire. After the nuts sat long enough to absorb the salt, we drained off the water and spread the peanuts on newspapers on the porch to dry.

After the war started, there were many soldiers in town on Saturdays from nearby Fort Stewart, 45 miles away, and from nearby army camps. We prepared boiled peanuts for my brothers to sell, filling small paper bags and packing them into their bicycle baskets. The boys rode into town and hawked their

wares, calling like circus barkers, "Boiled peanuts! Boiled peanuts! Five cents a bag!" I recently teased my brothers, noting
that although I helped with every step of the operation, I Don't
recall having received any remuneration. They just smiled with
satisfaction.

Cane grindings were social events in the fall. Farmers har-
vested the sugar cane when the leaves were beginning to turn
and there was a nip in the air. They often invited friends from
town to come and drink some of the delicious juice. A mule
pulled the winze around and around, endlessly, turning the
rollers through which the cane was fed to squeeze out the
juice. The juice was drained into a huge boiler where it cooked
for several hours over a fire. The person overseeing the cooking constantly skimmed off the foamy residue that rose to the
top, so that in the end, the beautiful, amber-colored syrup was
translucent. Folks stood around the cane grinding mill, visiting as they enjoyed the juice and the smoky smell of the
burning fire.

We usually butchered a hog when the weather turned cool
in the fall. I watched as they dipped the dead animal into boiling water, scraped the hair off, and hung it up on a scaffold. I
remember seeing Daddy slice the creature right down its front
and the steam rise as the warmth of the pig's insides met with
the cool air. I remember the particular, hot odor of the entrails
spilling out. It was not an unpleasant odor, just unique. The
men cut it into sections such as ham, shoulders, and bacon for
smoking; and I helped Mama in the kitchen, staying up until
midnight making and stuffing the sausage.

Mama made "hog's head cheese" the next day, boiling the
pig's brains, feet, some of the pork, gelatin, onions, and spices
together for several hours. Then she picked out what was edi-
ble, chopped everything up, molded it, and put it into the ice
box overnight to gel. Head cheese was considered a delicacy and
those who ate it said hers was the very best. It was served with
a touch of vinegar.

Mama became excited one afternoon when she saw what she thought were two wild turkeys light in a tree in the garden. With visions of turkey dinners on the table, she called to my brothers, "Boys, get the gun! Let's kill these birds." She was dipping the second one into the wash pot of boiling water when a neighbor, Mr. Womble, drove up. "Have you seen my pea-hens? They got out of the pen and flew off," he inquired. Mama wanted to crawl into that pot of hot water when she realized her mistake, and the neighbor wasn't very happy, either. Daddy paid the man $15 each for the fowl, which, as it turned out, were not turkeys at all and not good to eat. But it was worth the $30 for all the laughs we have had since.

Mama was active in church and community activities, though her work at home was burdensome. She washed clothes by hand, using a washboard and hung them on the clothesline to dry. She boiled the white things in the huge pot that was used to cook the cane juice into syrup when we had cane grindings. The nearby woodpile provided the fuel for the fire, as it did for the cook stove and one fireplace that were the only sources of heat during the winter.

Sometimes, Mama took the clothes to our neighbor's house to iron, using their electric iron rather than the "flat irons" at home that had to be heated by the fire. She paid Gladys 25 cents to cover the cost of electricity. While she ironed, I played with Gladys' daughters, Iva and Lucille, who were my only playmates. They had an authentic playhouse built by their Uncle George, a carpenter, who lived with them. We played with our dolls and played school, hospital, baby, "dress-up," and other dramas.

Transportation was a constant problem for Mama because we had only one vehicle, a Jeep or pickup truck that was usually in use on the farm. I believe Daddy could have been more accommodating about that, but she had good friends and neighbors who gave her a lift when she needed one.

An uncle, one of Daddy's brothers, came by one day, headed up country from the city. He stopped by just long enough to instruct Mama to have a bushel of green beans picked and ready for him to collect on his return home. Wordlessly, she did just that, walking to the back field and lugging the basket of beans back to the house. She was furious but would never have refused or complained to my uncle, who uttered not one word of thanks. It was a long, long time before I recognized my own pattern of self-sacrifice and silent suffering and learned on my own to say "no" and to set boundaries.

We know Mama was bright as the proverbial "light under a bushel," but she was self-effacing. In her 90s, long after she had retreated from the outside world, Mama could knock out a crossword puzzle in no time. Picking up her work later, I wondered how she knew some of the answers. I used to tell her she was pretty, but she always shrugged and denied it.

Through her women's church group, she studied a lot about the world and was president of the group more than once. She kept up with the latest homemaking tips, health, and food preparation and presentation through the Home Demonstration Club. She participated in the League of Women Voters, once helping in a campaign to prevent the county from going "wet."

She showed artistic talent in her childhood through her drawings but abandoned it later in life. When she was older and didn't go out, I tried to provide her with some supplies for drawing or painting, but she refused to consider it, as if she had already given up on living. The older she became, the more resentful and bitter she seemed and the more difficult it was to please her.

Our extended family was, well, extended, and was all very loving and complimentary toward me. At the huge family reunions on Daddy's side, I was often asked to entertain by reciting "readings". As a teenager, I began to rebel at being shown off in this way, so I hid in the car after the meal.

I knew almost all of my great-aunts and -uncles and second and third cousins and was close to all my first cousins. I looked forward to the many family get-togethers—Thanksgiving,

Christmas, New Year's, birthdays, annual reunions, and funerals even. I attended an all-night wake once with my mother where we sat up with the body right there in the living room.

I was asked to sing occasionally at the funeral of some relative, usually in a quartet. We sang a song once that was so mournful and archaic that my brother Gene, who always looked after me, warned me in a most emphatic way that he didn't want to hear of me singing such a song again.

Christmas was my favorite holiday, with family gatherings and treats that we did not have through the year—oranges, candy canes, hazelnuts, and things that "Santa" left. Having no electricity for tree lights, we hung a lot of icicles and some beautiful antique ornaments that sparkled in the light of the fireplace. Mama was sick one year on Christmas Eve, and little had been done to prepare for the holiday. Things were a mess—a pile of dirty clothes lay on the floor, and no special food had been prepared. Wanting so much to have a nice, festive house for Christmas, I frantically tried to straighten things up, with rather poor results as I recall.

Growing up on the farm, we had better food than money could buy but little that money could buy. I had never learned to like olives, for that reason. At a family gathering, a cousin once raved, "We're going to have olives with dinner!" and the others licked their lips at the thought. Fearing I was missing something, I slowly and carefully munched one of the things at each opportunity until I developed a taste for them myself. I could agree, finally, "We're going to have olives with dinner!"

Going to Savannah for the weekend was one of the highlights of my childhood. We visited my maternal aunts and uncles, my Granny and Grandpa Rushing, my cousins Barbara and Marilyn who lived with them, and my other cousin Eleanor. Mama and I rode the Trailways bus; some family member met us, or we took the city bus to Granny's. I giggled and grinned all of the 60 miles to the city. On the way, seeing people going about their business, I thought how lucky I was. *They're staying at home, and I'm going to Savannah!*

My grandparents were sweet to me, but preoccupied. I Don't remember having ever had a conversation with them; but my aunts and uncles were very loving and interested, which pleased Mama no end.

My Great-aunt, Nannie Kate Nelson, Grandmama Smith's youngest sister, was one of my dearest relatives. She loved everybody, children especially, playing patty cake with us and singing softly to us at night. She had scarlet fever as a child that settled in her ears and nasal passages, closing them up. Nan was nearly deaf as a result and had to breathe through her mouth. Over the years, she gradually developed a rather deformed appearance, with her head thrust forward, her back somewhat humped, and her mouth hanging open. But I had never noticed all this because I loved her so.

The school bus was stopped in town for a red light one day when I was in the seventh grade. Someone called out, "Hey, y'all! Look at that ugly woman!"

I looked and was shocked to see to whom it was they were pointing. *Why that's my Aunt Nannie Kate*, I thought. *I guess she does look rather odd.* But it didn't make any difference. I still loved her, and I cherish her memory to this day.

Mama's sister Matsy lived with my Granny and Grandpa in Savannah during the war years while her husband, Uncle Deal, was in the Navy. She had a strong influence upon me. Having no children of her own, she took an interest in her nieces and nephews, especially us girls. She was a grand Southern lady, was always dressed nicely, wearing stockings, even at the beach, and expected the house to be spotless at all times. We did a thorough cleaning job when she was coming to our house because we wanted to impress her favorably.

Daddy's sister, Nell, was my ideal woman, more open-minded and understanding than Aunt Matsy but equally refined. She always dressed sharply, was "hip," in no way prudish, and had a great sense of humor. I visited her and Uncle Olin and cousins Beth and Bill during two summers while in high school. They lived across the street from the city swimming pool where there was a cute lifeguard whom I dated when I visited there.

Nell was my second mother in my adult years when Mama was increasingly abusive. After being with Mama for a few days, I often went to Nell's to lick my wounds. In her letters, Nell wrote, "You are precious to me." It bruised my heart when she died at age 91 in a car crash.

Mama took food whenever we went to visit her relatives, in order to make up for any trouble or expense we might cause. When I was about 10, we traveled to Savannah where she had surgery on the varicose veins in her legs. She would have to stay in bed for a few days afterward, so she took me out of school to wait on her; saving her family the trouble of having to do so. If I disappointed her in some way, she would say, "What would the Savannah folks think?" What was the shame that drove her desperate need for approval, especially that of her family?

I seldom did babysitting because we lived out of town. On the few occasions when one of her friends called on me, Mama made sure that I didn't accept any payment, for these were her friends to whom she was indebted. I learned early what I lived—that my worth was based upon how good a showing I made, how hard I worked, and that approval was to be earned. In my book, *Love and Lemon Pie, Recipes for the Body and the Soul*, I wrote, "Someone has said there is only one kind of love—unconditional. Everything else is approval."

> **We don't need to be loved by everyone,
> so long as we're loved by someone.**

CHAPTER THREE

GROWING UP

I was domestic, and the house was extremely important to me. It was all Mama could do to take care of the washing and ironing, canning and cooking; so I was the main housekeeper. I battled with my brothers constantly to pick up after themselves until I finally devised a plan. I put any dirty boots found in the living room or clothes strewn on the floor into a barrel in the washhouse where the boys could go and retrieve them. It worked until they enlisted the support of my daddy, who ordered me to discontinue the practice.

I always had a playhouse, whether it was in the corner of the yard, in the barn, or in my room. My brothers tore it up on more than one occasion, out of mischief. I longed to have a real, permanent playhouse like my neighbors Iva and Lucille. Daddy told me, at last, that I could have the tiny chicken house in the back yard. I heated water on the wood stove in the kitchen and used it to scald the interior walls thoroughly, swept the dirt floor, and made curtains for the windows. It was a great place to be with my dolls and little kitchen.

Then Daddy told me a few weeks later that I would have to vacate, as he needed to use the building as a tool house.

I didn't mumble a word of protest, so he didn't realize how much it had meant to me. Ever since then, every house I have lived in has been my "playhouse."

My parents made a few modifications to our house when I was 12 or 13 so that I could have a room of my own. I painted the room with money that I had saved, made some window curtains, hung a wire across the corner for hanging clothes, and put up a curtain to hide all that. I believe my parents paid for the linoleum rug that they helped me put down on the wooden floor. How I loved having my own space.

I played school in my room, speaking the parts of the teacher and the students and rocked my dolls and put them to bed at night. I have a theory that play is where children develop verbal and conversational skills. In my day at least, girls' play involved dialog, whether it was hospital, wedding, school, or baby. On the other hand, boys' play was not so conversational as it was monosyllabic, as in, "Bang, you're dead!" or "Hands up! I got you covered!" or "You're out!"

As a counselor, I often discuss with my clients the difference between shame and guilt. Guilt, I believe, is about our behavior, and shame is about who we are and how others perceive us. I also believe shame is something we hide; it's what others Don't know about us.

Daddy took little pride or interest in the house, and long after we had electricity, we still had the outhouse. No amount of begging moved him to have an indoor bathroom put in. I was deeply embarrassed by the thing, which could be seen from the road, and it was especially mortifying when I began dating. I assumed, in fact, that there were certain boys who would not ask me out because of the house. This was more of an embarrassment than shame for me.

The real source of my shame, my secret, was something I couldn't speak of until years later. It was the fact that my parents obviously didn't love each other. Oh, how I longed for them to be more loving, and I looked for any sign of affection between them. Once, after Daddy had left to attend a national Farm Bureau convention in Chicago, Mama told me that he had actually kissed her goodbye. I was overjoyed, but she ridiculed my response and called me "silly."

Mama could cut one down in a flash with no concept of the hurt she had caused. She had many friends and cousins who thought she was sweet and wonderful, and anyone outside our immediate family always saw her in a good light. She was on her best behavior around her own siblings and cousins, who never felt the brunt of her insensitivity. But all Daddy had to do was walk into the kitchen for his lunch, and she pounced on him for one thing or another. He was a cute, quiet-spoken little guy and no match for her verbally. In later years, when he needed a rest in the afternoon, he laid down in the barn rather than go into the house. Daddy was kinder to me than Mama; and occasionally when she caused me to cry, he comforted me.

For his part, he got even with her in many passive-aggressive ways. He sometimes "accidentally" mowed over some of her precious shrubbery or "forgot" to pick up something at the grocery store in town. Once, on a Sunday morning, when it was time to leave for church, Mama was ready to go, dressed, with purse in hand. Daddy came in from the pasture about that time to get showered and dressed, making them late for the service.

"He does this to me every time!" she complained.

"Maybe he's getting even with you for something," I responded, trying to help her understand.

Puzzled, she protested, "I Don't know what he has to get even with me for."

Neither one of them understood what they were doing nor "got" what the other one was trying to say. And neither understood the price they paid. What a tragedy.

Daddy enjoyed life, though, and went his own way. He and his tractor were one. In later years, when returning from a trip with my brother Gene and his wife Brenda, he got on that tractor as soon as he could change clothes. He had many friends, old and young.

Mama criticized Daddy when he went into town to pay the electricity bill instead of mailing it. What she didn't know was that, the minute he walked in the door of an establishment and said, "Hello, you beautiful ladies," they fell all over themselves to take care of him. He had a habit of falling in love with any pretty woman, regardless of age, who smiled at him, and he made no effort to hide it. I don't know that he was actually unfaithful, but I know how it must have humiliated my mother. I remember how it embarrassed me.

Daddy was easier on me than Mama but was not very engaged in my everyday life. His time and energy went into eking out a living; and except for a movie in town now and then, he took little time for fun. He never went fishing, never played games with us, and joined only the church and Farm Bureau. He didn't talk to me much during my teen years or inquire about how things were going. He pretty much left it up to Mama to raise me, with few exceptions. It is likely that his lack of involvement was because he perceived that I was her ally; and perhaps it was true for a time as I was influenced by Mama's constant criticism of him. I said to him once, "Oh, Daddy, you're so cranky!" and wished later that I could take it back.

Daddy was hard on my brothers Gene and Jack. He gave them little understanding and, not knowing how to sit down and talk to them, he yanked off his belt and gave them a whomping for any and every infraction. Perhaps he took his anger at Mama out on the boys. He would never have dreamed that what he was doing would in the future be called abuse.

My brothers fought each other viciously, in turn, which frightened me terribly, and I often tried to break it up. The boys never seemed to hold a grudge about Daddy's abuse, surprisingly, and they were extremely kind and helpful as he grew older. I think he made up for his early abuse by being supportive of them as adults whenever one of them got into some sort of scrape. When he was very sick with cancer, Jack teased him, "Gene, don't you think now is the time to get even?" and Daddy replied, "Boys, I'm awfully sorry about that."

Mama was the counselor for a time for the Methodist Youth Fellowship that met on Sunday evenings before the church service. She gave me a part on the program one evening in the summer when I was about 13. As I stood before the group reading, I looked up and saw her standing in the back, scowling at me. I began to panic, shaking and struggling to catch my breath.

For weeks after that, the same terror came over me when I was called upon to read. I dreaded the time when I would be asked to read at school and panicked at the thought. There was no one to turn to for help.

I realized I couldn't go on like that and would have to think of a plan. The next time I was called upon, I took a deep breath and read very, very slowly to the end of the first sentence. I took another deep breath and after that, I felt relaxed. Over time, I overcame the trauma.

I was a late bloomer, the smallest girl in my class as a freshman, so was behind my classmates in "developing." When I asked my mother what Kotex™ was, she said, after a pause, "It means *sanitary.*" I knew she was lying because people don't whisper about "sanitary." She informed me, when I was nearing my 14th birthday, that before long I would begin to menstruate and showed me the supplies she had bought for me. She was proud that she had told me the "facts" since her mother had never told her. She had just begun her period without understanding what was happening and was so frightened that she hid in the outhouse all day.

She never talked to me about sex, on the other hand. As a young child, I asked her where babies came from; but she told me anything but the truth. I asked her one day about a visitor who was obviously far along in her pregnancy. Surely something was wrong with her! Mama hesitated and responded, "Well… she's sick."

I sat on the fence one afternoon, waiting to watch the veterinarian castrate some newborn male piglets. Dr. Barnes hesitated, looked over at Daddy, and said, "Thurmon," nodding toward me. "Peggy, go to the house," Daddy ordered. But never mind. I learned the "facts of life" from watching the animals on the farm. I surmised that, if that's what animals did, humans probably did it, too.

I was not allowed say "sex;" and when she heard the word, Mama made a face as if smelling some foul odor. I sat with some other young people one day, next to a boy who had his arm on the sofa behind me. Mama called me out of the room and instructed me not to allow it. No wonder I couldn't ask her what to do if a boy tried to kiss me. She had never dated anyone but Daddy; and she didn't kiss him until they were engaged, a rule she thought everyone should follow.

Daddy was more open-minded about love and sex. When I was about to marry, he confided in me about their lack of affection and sexual compatibility, blaming it on her. Who knows? I have often wondered what their wedding night was like, with each one as uninformed and insensitive as the other.

I didn't date until the boys my age had drivers' licenses since we lived out of town. In my senior year, I went steady with Charles, a good-looking boy who sat next to me in study hall. He and I did a lot of "smooching" that Mama never knew about. I loved kissing! Charles was captain of the football team, and I was a cheerleader. I still can hardly believe that Mama allowed me to wear that little short skirt and prance around all those boys.

Charles began pressuring me for sex after a while so that dating ceased to be any fun, and I had to break up with him in order to get relief. It's a good thing I kept the course because after I married, it took little effort to get pregnant.

Mama was extremely "modest" about the body; at least that was what she called it, while I call it "shame." I never saw her naked until she was old and frail and needed help with her bath. She didn't want me to attend swimming parties, so she told me that I didn't look good in a bathing suit, which was true. As an eighth-grader, I was the smallest girl in my class. When I did sprout, finally, my feet and hands grew first until I was the next-to-tallest girl when we graduated. The most comforting thing Mama ever said to me was, "Don't worry, your hands and feet feel awkward right now, but everything else will grow to match." And they did. All my girlfriends and classmates were wearing bras long before I even remotely needed one, and I was so undeveloped for so long that I prayed at night for God to give me breasts.

Mama also wanted me to be a "lady," which meant wearing shoes at all times. In order to prevent me from going barefoot, she told me that my feet were ugly. Actually, they weren't very pretty, but she made me self-conscious about it. Perhaps the reason I liked going without shoes is that, because of my flat feet, shoes were never very comfortable.

Mama saw that we had proper medical and dental care, a healthy diet, and decent clothes. I'm sure she scraped together the money to buy the *Lincoln Library*, a two-part set of books and later, the *Compton Encyclopedia*. She made sure we went to church and attended the youth group. I never felt embarrassed about my clothes, as many other people were at the same general socioeconomic level as we. We attended church and did business in town because we were close in, even though we lived on the farm and rode the school bus.

My closest girlfriends lived in town, and they certainly had nicer things than I did, but I was friendly with the students with whom I rode the bus and knew there were girls who had far less than I. Mama and I sewed many of my clothes, and it was not unusual in those days for us to make dresses out of feed sacks, not as primitive a practice as one might think. The sacks were actually made of printed material intended for sewing into garments. I took two years of home economics and learned to sew fairly well. By the time I was in high school, Daddy was making a little more money farming so that we could afford more purchases.

I had a long-running argument with Mama about nylon hose when I was 15. Most of the other girls started wearing them for church with pretty shoes instead of saddle oxfords and socks. I put in for hose, but Mama would hear none of it. She said I would look ridiculous wearing them on my skinny legs and must wait until I was 16. She didn't want me to wear lipstick, either, until age 16, but I solved that problem by waiting until I got on the school bus to apply it.

Sometimes, I invited my high school girlfriends out to swim in the pond and ride the horse. Gene and Jack built a little cabin close to the pond with bunk beds and a potbelly stove. We girls spent the night there sometimes, with me doing the planning and cooking for the group. My brothers came after we were in bed, raining buckets of rocks on the roof or making eerie noises to try to spook us. They were such rascals, but they would say that I deserved it for some odd reason.

I learned to swim in the fishpond with Gene as my instructor. He dragged me, screaming, to the middle of the pond, turned me loose, and said, "Sink or swim." I dog- paddled to the edge, and after I got my breath, he pulled me out into the middle again.

Mama could hear me screaming. "I don't understand why you go down there with them if that's the way they treat you," she said when I got to the house. I explained that if I didn't go with them, I wouldn't get to go swimming at all. I learned some other strokes on my own eventually, and became quite a good swimmer.

It seemed to me that my parents cared more about how I *looked* than about how I *was*. I've always tilted my head and was in college before discovering the cause—double vision that I was born with. Even my baby pictures show my little head leaning to one side. Daddy especially hated it. He scolded me and told me, "You'd be the finest girl in the world if you would just hold you head straight." He sometimes slipped up behind me, as I practiced piano, grabbing my head, and demanding, "Straighten up that head!"

Yet, tilting my head compensated for the double vision, and it was hard to remember to keep it straight. I have repeatedly been misjudged by people who interpret this as "body language," a sign of lack of self-confidence, coquettishness, or by other wives as flirtatiousness. When, at age 61, I had eye surgery to correct the problem, my mother didn't ask, "How do you see now?" She asked, "How do you look now?"

I learned to drive around the farm long before age 16, but Daddy did not allow me to drive on the highway until I had a license. On the day of my 16th birthday, to the courthouse I went to take the driving test. This was before the introduction of driver education in school, and I had never laid eyes on a driving manual. A cute state trooper stood over me and told me the answers on the written test. I passed.

Camp meetings, held each summer for a week, were popular during those days and are still in operation, though the attendance is sparser now. I'm not sure how many are still in operation. Our Methodist camp meeting still is held at the Tattnall Camp Ground, just two miles from the "Home Place." Four services are held each day, beginning with Morning Watch at 7:00, an 11:00 A.M. service, one at 3:00 P.M. and another at 7:00 in the evening. People who didn't "tent" come out during the day or evening to attend what services they can. The meetings are held under a large shelter called the "tabernacle," which could be plain or made with beautifully carved beams. In the early days, families lived in tents for the week and later built cabins and cottages as they could afford them. The cabins are arranged in a square with the tabernacle in the center.

Most of my relatives and forefathers renewed their faith at "altar calls" when the preacher invited them to come and rededicate their lives to "Jesus Christ as your Lord and Savior." A special preacher was engaged for the week-long event and was usually more evangelistic in style than our local pastor.

I attended camp meeting every summer until I married and moved away. I went home during camp meeting the summer of 2000 to attend with Daddy, not knowing it would be his last summer. I longed to go to the altar, as I had in the past, and feel some special inspiration. But the minister gave a pretty weak invitation, compared to the old days, and I was one of only a dozen people who knelt there. I suppose it's true that we can't go back.

It doesn't matter what your circumstances are;
what matters is what you make of them.

CHAPTER FOUR

COLLEGE

I had planned to attend a small teacher's college not far from home, but my pastor urged me to attend LaGrange College instead. It was a small Methodist-related school in LaGrange, Georgia, in the northwestern part of the state. It had a more spiritual atmosphere but was much more expensive; and I rejected his suggestion several times, assuming we couldn't afford it.

I asked Mama what she thought; and she suggested I ask Daddy, who agreed to it. He dug up some sweet potatoes to pay for the first half of that semester's tuition and sent the rest when he had the money. He didn't have to sign any promissory note, any contracts or agreements. It was that informal and intimate. Off I went at the end of the summer, two weeks after my 17th birthday.

It was my oyster. The freshman class lived upstairs in Smith Hall, the original and only building when the school was founded in 1831 as a girls' school. I understand that it was the first college in the state and was one of the first women's colleges in the country. Smith Hall served as the administration building and freshman dorm and had the kitchen and dining room in the basement. The president's office was directly under my corner room, which was large, with a high ceiling and four large windows. My roommate, Patty Deal, and I walked to town, purchased some bright red-and-yellow plastic curtains for the windows and otherwise decorated the room rather nicely. There was a common bathroom with showers and a telephone in a closet in the hall.

Uncle Deal, my Aunt Matsy's husband, was the band, orchestra, and choir director at the high school and taught violin at the

college in the afternoons. He was on the faculty of the college, therefore, and the college faculty was aware that I was Matsy's niece. Patty was Uncle Deal's niece. Matsy was Mama's sister while Uncle Deal was Patty's mother's brother. Patty and I were not actually kin but were about the same height and coloration, and people couldn't tell us apart. We both showed up our first week with identical dresses, as if things weren't confusing enough. There were some teachers on the staff who never could tell us apart. The biology teacher, years later, still asked, "Now, are you Patty or Peggy?

We were always short of men performers for the theater and choir programs and borrowed talent from the high school programs when possible. Our director and Uncle Deal were good friends and worked cooperatively together, so we borrowed one of Uncle Deal's tenors to be the leading man in our spring operetta. That was fine, until dress rehearsal night. It coincided with Uncle Deal's own dress rehearsal at the high school. The defiant young man knew where his obligation was—Uncle Deal's chorus—but for some reason, chose to attend our rehearsal instead.

Patty and I were standing on the front row of the chorus when we saw our uncle barge into the auditorium through the back door. We watched him march down the aisle like a storm trooper and bend over "Madame," our director, who was sitting in the director's chair. I could feel my face growing hot with embarrassment and wanted to sink into the floor as I heard him bark at "Madame, you've a lot of guts to take my tenor away!"

Madame made no response but continued to direct the song.

Patty was equally mortified.

I called Uncle Deal afterward and told him that he owed Madame an apology, but he claimed he was in the right. I protested to Dr. Henry, the president, also, but he defended Deal. Aunt Matsy never mentioned it, but I'm sure she knew about it and was sorely embarrassed.

We recalled that night when I ran into that same young man—now in his late sixties—at my class reunion three years ago. "That's the worst career mistake I ever made," he said. "Mr. Deal never forgave me for my disloyalty, and I have never forgiven myself."

Many receptions were held and much courting was done in the elegantly furnished parlor on the first floor. The front porch with its white columns and big rocking chairs is still the college emblem on all its literature. Smith Dorm faced the quadrangle, along with Banks Library, Hawks Building—which contained classrooms and dorm rooms for sophomores—and Dobbs Auditorium—which contained classrooms, labs, and music rooms. I minored in pipe organ, and it was in Dobbs that I played for daily chapel on a big organ from silent movie days. It still had all the original sound effects, including sleigh bells, drums, whistles, and an eerie "vox humana." I Don't think I was all that talented; I just worked hard, practiced long hours, and my fellow students were very accepting.

Our freshmen housemother was a young widow who lived in the largest room with her young daughter, Donna. Donna was somewhat of a pest, threatening to report any infraction to her mother.

For our part, we tormented her. When we told her frightening stories and accused her of doing disgusting things, she shrank in fright and went running to her mother.

I don't know who it was that rolled a crate of Coke bottles down the stairs during the night or broke into the kitchen for a late night snack. As for me, I liked to lean out the window about bedtime and moo like a cow. I sat on the fire escape a few times and took a puff or two on a cigar.

I joined the choir first semester and the Curtain Raisers, the second. To audition for this drama group, I had to read a script, ad lib, and give a reading of my own. I gave a piece in Italian dialect about "Giuseppe the Barber," and the roomful of people roared with laughter as I rolled my eyes and described Giuseppe's "da beega, da blacka mustache." I easily made it into the Curtain Raisers.

Celebration!

The choir went on tour during spring break every year, visiting churches and schools mostly. We wore evening dresses in pastel colors for the evening programs and sang religious and popular songs. Miss Elizabeth Gilbert, or "Madame" as we called her, was our beloved director and much respected throughout the state. Dr. Henry accompanied us for the purpose of public relations; and Mr. Austin Cook, the business manager whom we called "Cookie," came along to pay the bills. I believe one important reason for their presence on the tour was that they liked being around us girls, and we loved having them.

A young man in the audience at one of the high schools, seeing our chorus of pretty maidens, called out, "You mean they can sing, too?"

Patty and I stored our belongings at the end of our freshman year in an unlocked closet in a corner room in Hawks Dorm and left them there for the summer. Patty transferred to the University of Georgia after two years, and Mattie became my roommate. We asked "Cookie" to save us a corner room at the end of each semester, where we left our things until fall.

Rules were strict. One was allowed to smoke only with permission from home and then only in a designated "smoker." Anyone caught smoking without permission received a "call down," a written record of an infraction of any kind. Three call-downs equaled a "campus," which meant we couldn't leave the campus for a certain length of time. We were still in the Deep South where proper women didn't smoke or drink—as least, not publicly.

I was a religion major and didn't want to be seen as "holy," so I slipped into the smoker occasionally, borrowed a cigarette, and took a few puffs. I'm sure that I didn't come across as all that cool because I choked every time.

We weren't allowed to attend class or be on the quadrangle in shorts, gym suits, or jeans even. We had to wear a raincoat over our shorts if we had class following gym. We were not allowed to wear curlers to the dining room where all our meals except breakfast were served family style. We dressed in evening dresses for dinner once a month and celebrated birthdays for that month.

We were not allowed to have a car on campus until the second semester of our senior year, but that was no big deal because few students could afford a car of their own anyway. We walked the two miles to town often to see a movie, get a hamburger afterward, and do any shopping. The college became co-ed just before I entered; and there were no men's dorms yet, so most of the men students were "town boys" on the maintenance staff who had cars. This came in handy at times. The college, called "The Hill," was the highest point in the city; and climbing it was quite arduous after we walked all the distance from town. I walked up the driveway backwards to save my leg muscles.

The education majors did practice teaching when we were second-semester seniors, for which they could use a college car. Sam, one of our most daring and entertaining classmates, drove one of the cars. She and some other imps had a spare key made and saved it for the opportune time when they could sneak out after hours and go for a spin. Alas, the night watchman caught them and brought them before Dr. Henry. Sam figured that having had the key made sounded rather premeditated and therefore a more serious crime than the story she made up. She explained that she had simply hot-wired the car and hoped Dr. Henry wouldn't ask her to demonstrate. I don't remember what their punishment was, but I don't think it was serious. Dr. Henry may have even been amused, anyway. We laughed about this at our 50th reunion in 2004.

Miss Irene Annette was our excellent drama director who could blow up in a split second over who-knows-what. She called it "artistic temperament." We stopped often to watch the fountain on the square on our trips to town. We took in the calm intervals for a few minutes until suddenly, one great geyser blasted into the sky. We laughed and shouted, "There goes

Celebration!

Miss Annette!" We accepted that part of her, though, appreciated what we learned from her, and loved her greatly.

I had a wonderful time in college and was quite the social butterfly. Perhaps it was because I never had a sister that my dorm mates meant so much to me. We could find someone to snuggle up with if one of us wasn't feeling well during the night. Homosexuality was not a blatant issue in those days, so we were free to be close.

We gathered in someone's room sometimes at night after study hall. We did each other's hair, chattered about boys, marriage and sex, our wedding night, and otherwise cut up. Miss Miller, our English teacher and housemother who lived in the dorm, came knocking at the door after a while; and no matter whose room we were in, she said, "Peggy, you girls need to quiet down." Did my voice carry that well, or did she simply assume I was in the middle of whatever was going on?

A couple got married in the chapel on campus occasionally, with Dr. Henry performing the ceremony. Some of us gathered on the steps of Pitts Dorm one evening at about 10:30 and conjectured as to what the newlyweds might be doing about that time. As far as I knew, very few of us engaged in sex before marriage. Remember this was before "the pill," so while we thought we were being moral, perhaps we were simply being safe.

Dr. Melson, our religion professor, was a fatherly type who had great confidence in me. He pushed me to get all the experiences I could. And I did. I took part in a "fellowship team" sponsored by the Methodist Conference for college students the summer after my freshman year, when I was still 17. After a week's training, I went with the rest of my team, made up of an adult advisor and three other students, to work in churches in rural southern Georgia, helping to organize and revitalize youth programs.

We stayed one week in each community and, on Saturday, transferred to a new assignment, where we were usually on the program for the Sunday service. We lived in the homes of the church members and ate supper at a different home every evening, with lunch at the church. We kept track of the number of times we had fried chicken—25 out of 30 meals; but we didn't object, for serving fried chicken meant the hostess was serving us her very best. I loved those country, salt-of-the-earth folks and was sorry when we left each Saturday for a new destination.

When I returned to college in the fall, I told Dr. Melson what a wonderful time I had and that I wanted to do the same thing the following summer. He said, "No, you must spread your wings. Next summer, you must go on a Methodist Youth Caravan." It was a program similar to the one I had just completed but was national. Of the five training centers in the United States, the center we chose for training determined where we spent the summer. I chose the training farthest away—California—in order to have a greater adventure. I traveled by Greyhound Bus from Georgia to Stockton, California, with two other girls.

After a week of training, I joined a team of three young women and one young man with a darling older woman as our advisor. I married this young man, whom I will call Thomas, two years later. We were assigned to Long Beach, Lancaster, Hemet, and other communities in the desert near Tehachapi. In Lancaster, I slept in the room of a teenage boy who was away for the summer. His collection of model airplanes hung from the ceiling, and one morning, I awoke to see them flying in formation. We were having an earthquake.

During our ride to California, I learned that one of the other girls had spent the previous summer on a caravan in Cuba. I had always heard about the Cuba Caravan, which was sponsored by the Georgia and Florida conferences, and thought it sounded exciting. This was 1952 B.C.—before Castro. At that time, Cuba was a part of the Florida Conference and had an American District Superintendent. I determined at that moment that I would be on the Cuba Caravan the following summer.

Thomas and I did not become romantic that summer; but I liked his gentility, his values and life goals. His father, brothers, and several uncles were ministers, and his grandfather had been a bishop in China—impressive—and he himself planned to go into the ministry. He had already committed to spend the next summer in France on a World-Council-of Churches-sponsored work camp, and I was certain I was going to Cuba.

I learned from one of my teammates that he "liked" me, but he never gave any indication. We corresponded the following year, and he visited me at my college. I thought he would never kiss me; but the second night, he finally got up the courage to do so. I attended his graduation in Indiana, and we made a commitment to continue the relationship seriously.

Dr. Howard Worth came to teach religion in our sophomore year. He was not the fatherly type like Dr. Melson and was more demanding. "Of all your college experience, what was of greatest value?" he asked me, ten years after I graduated. I had to ponder this question for a while.

"You forced me to think," I wrote him later.

The first course I took with him was "Worship," and the main topic of the course was the question, "What kind of God do we worship?"

Dr. Worth was a Connecticut Yankee and had no taste for our Southern ways, especially our segregation rules and form of worship. He challenged everything I had ever taken for granted. He ridiculed some of the songs we sang in our Sunday evening services—they really did express some pretty bad theology and were equally bad musically—and he generally stirred things up.

I don't believe I had ever thought deeply about the issues he brought up. I was thoroughly confused and hated his guts for a while. However, while not instructing me in *what* to think, he led me in the experience of questioning everything I had mindlessly bought into, unexamined. Now my beliefs and values were my own—not hand-me-downs. It was painful but profitable, and I thanked him many times.

I still had to apply and be interviewed by the committee for the Cuba Caravan. I went by bus to Atlanta for the occasion, and they accepted me on the spot. I called my dorm mates from the bus station, declaring, "I'm going to Cuba!" and they were delighted for me.

I remember the day we arrived in Havana from Miami, where I had teamed up with students from other states. Some of them were to be in a work camp and some on another caravan. Sam Laird from the church headquarters in Nashville met us at the airport and when I saw him, I exclaimed, "Sam, this is the happiest day of my life!" He drove us to the bus station where a bus transported us across the island to a Methodist college, Colegio Pinson in Camaguey, our training center. (I see from the internet that this church-related college no longer exists). We ate a meal of *arroz con pollo* (chicken and rice) while waiting for the bus to leave; and long after its departure time, we finally got under way. We had a week of training, including sensitivity to the culture and customs. This was long before "sensitivity training."

I was assigned, once again, to a team made up of three college women and one young man and an adult advisor. My teammates were Jorge—a medical student, Ondina, Cathy—who was from Illinois, and Almaida, our adult advisor. We were assigned to the eastern province of Oriente, which was mountainous, rural, and beautiful.

Again, we lived in the homes and were fed by church members. We spent some afternoons visiting members of the community and sometimes met with the leaders of the youth groups, teaching them to plan, organize, and lead programs. We worked with any available adult advisors as well.

One of my favorite places that we served was a small village in the mountains where there was a tiny chapel made of local materials, including a roof of palm branches and a dirt floor. We stayed in the small home of the young lay pastor and his wife and two young children; and from their house, we looked out over a vast expanse of valley with gorgeous tropical plants and trees.

Celebration!

Revolution was in the air in 1953, and there was a scuffle in the mountains near us, in which 17 of Batista's soldiers and several revolutionaries were killed. I realized several years later that this was the beginning of Castro's revolution.

Soldiers stood in the back of the room when we had meetings at the churches to make sure we were not helping plot a revolution. Armed men stopped us and searched our suitcases when we moved from one assignment to another. Cathy once attempted to take a snapshot of the incident, but a soldier sternly warned her stop or he would smash her camera. I found this all very exciting. As we drove off, I looked back to see this same solder blow me a kiss.

Our next assignment was a church in the small town of Buenaventura where the pastor, Mario Fernandez, had just broken up with his fiancé. He confided to my American team member that he was attracted to me, and I felt some attraction, too, but none of this was ever overt because he knew of my commitment to Thomas, who was in France.

My Cuban friends described their suffering under the dictator Batista, and I was pleased a few years later when I first heard of Castro and the news that the revolution had taken place. I even thought that in the future, I might return to the island as a missionary. I grieved when I learned that, after the Revolution, Mario was imprisoned and tortured by the Castro government. I never heard from him again. I was further disillusioned by news that I heard, first hand, of the cruelties committed by Castro and of his failure to form a democracy.

We rode to a new assignment each Saturday, sometimes by car, sometimes by bus, and once by rail-section car, one of those little cars used by a section foreman and his crew. This one had no motor, so the crew had to pump it to make it go.

There were few amenities and no stores in one small village where we spent just a couple of days. We had been advised never to drink anything but bottled water or soda pop unless it was a hot drink such as coffee or tea. At one of the homes where we ate, I noticed some pigs playing in a puddle near the well from which the drinking water was drawn and declined the glassful that was offered at dinner, but my teammate Cathy had forgotten. She gulped down a big swallow before I could stop her. The next day, she was quite sick, but thank goodness we were back in town and could get some help. My stomach must be made of cast iron because I didn't get sick all summer.

This was a rural area, and most people were quite poor; so the basic menu was rice and beans with plenty of tree-ripened pineapple, bananas, papaya, and avocados. We didn't eat anything that wasn't recently cooked or peeled. I loved the food, eating heartily, so that I added some inches to my hips by the time I returned home. We were once housed in the back of a small church, where the church young people brought us breakfast of *cafe con leche* (coffee with milk) and freshly made bread with butter each morning. Cathy didn't care for it and gave me her share, which I ate up.

The communities where we served were Mayarí, Baguanos, Preston, Buenaventura, Omaja, and Nuevitas, with side trips to small missions in Felton and Guaro and to the Methodist Agricultural Industrial School in Mayarí. We "caravaners" walked the young people home after our program was finished in the evenings, singing and talking as we made our way through the village or town. This was one of the most meaningful things we did, in my opinion.

I studied Spanish in high school and college and spoke enough to get by, but there were times when it wasn't adequate. One morning, as I was about to leave for the day from the home where I was staying, the hostess told me that the caravan was invited for "marienda."

I asked, "Que es marienda?" (What is *marienda?*)

She replied that it was lunch, *por la tarde.*

I thought "la tarde" meant "evening." So, when I returned at about 6:00 P.M. to bathe and change, the daughter asked me, "Peggy, *Donde estaba la caravana?*" (Where was the caravan?)

Celebration!

"Ellos vienen ahora," (They're coming now.) I answered.

Alarmed, she ran into the kitchen, calling, "Mama, Mama!"

I discovered that they had expected us for afternoon tea, and now we were all coming for dinner instead. Graciously, they put on another pot of rice, so there was plenty for all. They teased me, and we all had a good laugh.

While I can't brag about my Spanish, I spoke with good accent because Professor Hamph, our Spanish teacher at college, had drilled us mercilessly in pronunciation. I had become quite tan in the tropical sun; and many times, if I refrained from talking too much, people thought I was from Havana.

Mama enjoyed hearing of my adventures when I returned home at the end of the summer, about my team brother and sisters and the people with whom we had worked. We laughed heartily when I tried to teach her to roll her "r's" in Jorge's name.

I was asked to speak about my experience in Cuba when I returned to college in September. I was president of three campus organizations that year, not a good idea, because it took away from my studies. The main organization that I led was the YWCA, which had an active program.

One of our fundraisers was "Suppressed Desires Day." By paying 50 cents, a person could purchase a tag permitting one to chew gum in class, wear curlers and jeans anywhere on campus, take pillows and teddy bears into class, sit at the faculty tables in the dining room, and call the faculty members by their first names. In turn, the faculty could cut in line at the cafeteria. I still have the clipping from the city newspaper describing the occasion and a picture of me wearing a skirt with my feet propped up on Dr. Henry's desk. He's the one who called the reporter and I have good reason to think he enjoyed the scene.

Thomas planned to visit me over Christmas, at which time we would announce our engagement. I was distressed about the outhouse and dreaded for him to see it. I worried about his parents coming for the wedding in the summer. They were cultured city folk, and I could imagine how shocking it would be for them and unbearably humiliating for me. But I said nothing, assuming it would do no good.

When I arrived home for Thanksgiving, however, there it was, a bathroom, installed on the back porch! I can't describe how delighted and relieved I was. When I saw it, I knew that my brother Gene had built it for me, especially, and over Daddy's objections. The water heater came from the old dairy barn that hadn't been used for years, but Daddy opposed the project.

"I may need to use it again one of these days," he complained.

I realized that Gene was as ashamed of the old outhouse as I was and remembered that he had always looked after me, his little sister. That's how I knew that he was the one who had installed the bathroom. I will forever be grateful.

I had the leading role in a play, *The Happiest Years*, in my senior year, even though I was not a drama major. I played a mother-in-law who continually fussed over her sansevieria plant, the name of which ironically translates as "mother-in-law's tongue." My years of experience in the Curtain Raisers were great fun, whether I played a role or was on the crew. The bonds that we forged in six weeks of rehearsal were strong.

Representatives of the Junior Chamber of Commerce in LaGrange approached me toward the end of my senior year and invited me to be in the Miss LaGrange Pageant. It was the predecessor to the Miss Georgia Pageant in Columbus, Georgia, and of course, the Miss America Pageant. Dr. Henry recommended me, and my talent would be the pipe organ.

My organ teacher discouraged me from entering because of her assumption that the instrument provided would not be a pipe organ but something less adequate for my piece, Bach's "Cathedral Prelude in E-Minor." My main concern was that I would have to walk across the stage in a bathing suit. What would Mama say? In those days the suits were all one piece and very modest compared to the ones these days. But I remembered her concern with modesty and dreaded her criticism.

Celebration!

Thomas was also objecting to it; and I gathered from his comments that he feared that, if I did succeed in the pageant, I would change my mind about marrying him. He was getting some support for this position from skeptical classmates.

The Jaycees assured me that they would have the Columbus club put a clause into the contract stating that they would furnish a concert model Hammond, which could accommodate the footwork my piece called for. I gave in, finally, taking the chance that it would work out with Mama and Thomas.

The LaGrange Pageant went well, and I won.

My chaperone and I traveled to Fort Benning in Columbus for the next stage. The Jaycees spent a lot of money for my wardrobe, and I chose a pattern for a dress that I could wear for the pageant and modify for my wedding later in the summer. It was made of Avalon lace over white satin, and the skirt was covered with 350 rhinestones. Had I won the Miss Georgia event, my wedding would have been postponed for a year.

The pageant took place on two separate evenings; the first was the talent part. I suggested we check out the organ before going in for dinner that first evening. There stood a small "field model" instrument with two half-keyboards and eight pedals, to our dismay. Alarmed, we went straight to the director of the pageant and told him that it was impossible for me to give my performance on the thing. His only response was a weak, "Well, I'm sorry." I would be eliminated that very first evening without performing. There had been bad blood between the LaGrange Jaycees and those in Columbus. Was this intentional sabotage?

My chaperone went straight to the telephone and called the Jaycees president in LaGrange to report the problem. We attended the dinner, not knowing what my fate would be. When we returned to the backstage at the auditorium, we saw a concert model Hammond being plugged in, two minutes before the start of the pageant. I played well enough that night and appeared in my evening gown later in the evening.

The second night included the swimsuit competition and the interviews. I will always regret not doing better on the interview—I, a college senior, who could think on my feet and speak so well. It was not that I was nervous; it was that I was not prepared. We had spent too much time on my wardrobe and appearance and failed to go over possible questions, practicing meaningful responses. I berated myself for years. How I wished I could redo those 15 minutes. I was third runner up.

My picture appeared in the Atlanta paper later that summer, along with the story, "The Missing Pipe Organ."

Thomas and I had planned to spend the summer in a "Students in Industry" project for college students in the Minneapolis-St. Paul area. It included working in a factory and serving in a ministry for the employees, but we decided against it for financial reasons. Thomas spent the summer with us on the farm, living in a shack by the pasture, working at a tobacco warehouse, and helping with the youth program at my church on weekends. My mother, several of her friends, and I prepared for the wedding and removed the 350 rhinestones from my dress. There was much excitement in the air.

Spread your wings!

CHAPTER FIVE

MARRIAGE, SCHOOL, AND THE MINISTRY

I had been groomed by my church and by my mother to marry a minister—not to *be* one mind you, but to marry one. Mama had always idolized the preacher, and the preacher's wife and schoolteachers were my only role models. Besides, Mama had insisted that I marry a man who was the opposite of Daddy and the boys, someone more cultured and genteel. As it turned out, I married somebody very much like her.

Apparently, Thomas met every requirement. He was scholarly, polished, and was preparing for the ministry. He was athletic, spoke and wrote well, and I liked his values, goals, and social consciousness and felt a lot of affection for him. He didn't have the good looks I would have preferred, but I reasoned that his looks were not as important as his other qualities. Thomas and I would surely have a wonderful life in the ministry and go to the mission field in addition.

Best of all, when he made Bishop, Mama would surely be proud. Then she could brag about her son-in-law the Bishop, and I would finally have her approval.

Mama was favorably impressed. When she talked with Thomas' mother on the phone the first time, she declared, "Thomas is a prince!" My brothers accused her of being more in love with him than I. Perhaps we were both "in love" with who we thought he was.

Beneath the facade though, he was different; and it didn't take long after I was married for Mama to express her disappointment—with him and with me. I tried to defend him, a behavior that I was to engage in for many years.

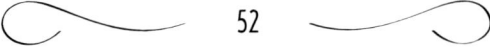

In case I had been impressed by the attention I had gotten as a participant in the Miss Georgia Pageant, Thomas reminded me that looks were not important. I ignored some of his confusing behaviors, which grew more obvious as the wedding day approached. Well, yes, I saw them but didn't realize the significance because I didn't know what was normal and didn't understand that I could back out. As Clarissa Pinkola Estes said in the Bluebeard story in *Women Who Run with the Wolves*, "This error of judgment is almost routine in a woman so young that her alarm systems are not yet developed." Besides, the gifts had started to arrive, the beautiful dress was ready, and too many people were impressed by my "catch" to disappoint them. Worst of all, Mama would be disappointed. So the preparations continued.

Slowly, methodically, he tightened his grip. He was jealous of a 14-year-old boy from the church youth camp who grabbed my hand and hung onto it. He was suspicious whenever I hugged any man and disapproved of a snapshot that made me look bustier than I was. He demanded that I turn over to him what little money I had and insisted that I shampoo his hair and polish his shoes. I willingly complied. It was not long after our marriage that I began to wonder if I had made a mistake, but I believed that I could fix it by trying harder. After all, we were going into the ministry.

I understood intuitively that it was my job to make him adequate, just as I had with my mother. This was not an uncommon assumption among ministers and their wives. Another minister's wife, learning that I had majored in religion and minored in organ and theater, said, "My, what a help you are to your husband!" And I tried to be.

We were married in August in my home church, surrounded by many friends and a multitude of relatives. Between my pastor, Shannon Holloway, Thomas's father, who was a minister, Vernard Robertson, one of my former pastors, and a groomsman friend of Thomas's who was a seminary student, there were five preachers in the wedding. Thus, we were thoroughly married after reciting from memory the vows we had written. The ceremony was beautiful, with my attendants dressed in white, carrying corsages of red carnations, and the men in white summer tuxedoes with red carnation boutonnières.

Afterwards, we left for a two-day honeymoon at St. Simon's Island where we could relax before packing our belongings and heading to Boston where Thomas was in school. On the wedding night, I was confused and disappointed to discover that Thomas had neglected to make a trip to the drug store and was not prepared for the "consummation" of our marriage. It was understood that we would use protection.

I wondered, "*Was he too embarrassed to make the purchase or just not interested?*

After our return home, we headed for Boston in the used car we had purchased with the money from my Miss LaGrange winnings. Because we had little money for meals and hotels, our honeymoon was a camping trip. My cousins teased me about wearing those fancy nightgowns in a pup tent. We purchased a charcoal grill and scrounged a few pans left from my brothers' Boy Scout days but little else—and we had little experience in the art of camping. We had difficulty getting a fire started in the grill, the car sometimes wouldn't start, and Thomas was aggravated and cross with me for much of the trip. The verbal abuse, which was to last for 24-½ years, began. As for me, I either pouted or tried to placate his unhappy mood.

Once in Boston, we prepared for the fall semester. I found an office job at Boston University, close to our married students' apartment building and close to Thomas's school. I typed papers and exams for the chairman of the government department and five professors who were not easy to please. Thomas and I directed a church youth program at a suburban church on weekends, where I taught the Sunday School class of junior high school youth while Thomas took the seniors, and we both planned and directed the Sunday evening programs.

I typed, edited, and revised Thomas's papers, sometimes staying up late at night.

We took a busload of our high school students to New York during Christmas break, visited the Abyssinian Baptist Church in Harlem, and saw the movie *Cinderella* and the Rockettes at Radio City Music Hall.

On Saturday afternoons, we met with the head pastor for planning and supervision, the time of the week I dreaded most. He and Thomas did not get along; and on those occasions, I sat and watched, distraught, while the two of them wrangled about any and everything for an hour and a half. I think that Thomas's red hair and ruddy complexion often betrayed his anger and hostility, causing even more negativity from the other party. I desperately took my husband's side, trying to defend him. How I detested Saturdays!

For the spring semester, I was awarded a grant to attend school at Boston University to earn a master's degree in drama. When Thomas declared that I was not to play any romantic role and that I was certainly not to kiss a man in such a role, I felt that my possibilities would be limited. I felt quite lost in the big school anyway, having come from a small college and entering the program second semester after all the others had become oriented in the fall. In February, I discovered I was pregnant and was not feeling well, so I dropped out of school, assuming that this was as far as I would go with my own education. Besides, the prospect of becoming a mother pleased me more than getting a master's degree.

An early experience describes the loneliness that I experienced for many years. We had been married for six months, and I was three months pregnant when we attended a weekend retreat for young couples. That night, the women slept on cots on a balcony overlooking an open area below where the men slept. At bedtime, I watched Thomas as he prepared for bed, slowly and methodically arranging his bedding and himself. I couldn't call to him, so I waited, wishing that he would look up and wave goodnight or nod or—just look up. It would have been unlike him to throw a kiss. Finally, as if he had forgotten I was there, he pulled up the covers and went to sleep.

In keeping with the traditions of the day, I would not work after the baby came, so we moved during the summer to the town of Eliot in southern Maine. It was near Kittery, Maine, just over the New Hampshire state line. There we served a small church while Thomas commuted to and from school in Boston, which was not far on the turnpike. Our parsonage was big and drafty and would take a large percentage of our meager salary to heat it to a livable temperature. But it was a charming New England-style house only a brisk walk from the church, which was on the edge of town and served the surrounding semi-rural area.

Mark was born in October at Boston's Beth Israel Hospital, where I had received prenatal care. I returned to Boston to give birth shortly before the baby was due and stayed with friends. I woke up with labor pains on Sunday morning, October 16, 1955, and Mark was born that afternoon. I was given spinal anesthesia and a "twilight" drug so that I did not remember one thing about his birth and did not get to hold him until evening. I felt sorely cheated by not being involved in his birth and by not having been able to hold him sooner. I had to lie flat of my back for several hours each day because of a head-ache from the spinal anesthesia. Some of our church members helped take care of Mark and me after we returned to Maine. He was a healthy, happy, and beautiful baby. Now I had a real-live doll to play with! One of my most precious memories is of a social occasion at the church. One of the ladies held Mark as I watched him from across the room. Then, seeing me through the crowd, he smiled!

Some of our members lived on the road leading from town, past our house and to the church. Many of the families had lived in this community for generations; and being New England Yankees, they were a tight-knit group and not quick to open their doors to strangers. But as the pastor and family, we had an immediate "in" and were welcomed and embraced. I often pushed Mark in the stroller through the snow to join neighbors for "koffee klatch." Lorin and Ima Clingman, a retired couple with no children, lived next door on a hill and occasionally kept Mark while we made pastoral visits. The high school kids got off the school bus at our house sometimes to play with Mark, and our house was used as a nursery during church services.

We became close friends with a few couples, including Gordon and Carolyn Johnson. Gordon ran a small grocery store and meat Market, describing himself as a "meat man." We lured Gordon to our church to establish and lead a choir when we learned that he was musical and could sing. He came and stayed with the church long after we moved on. He and Carolyn and their five children became an integral part of the fellowship.

We were not far from an Air Force base in Portsmouth, New Hampshire, just over the river from where we lived. A Strategic Air Command unit was being installed at the base, and service men and women were being transferred there in great numbers. There were no quarters for married couples, only barracks for singles. Many residents recognized an opportunity when they saw one and began to put rooms or apartments up for rent. When the face of the person ringing the doorbell was brown, however, the room had suddenly "been taken." Signs went up in the barbershops: "We reserve the right to refuse service."

Renting a room would help with our heating bill, and after clearing it with the Board, we decided to let out an upstairs bedroom. One of the questions on the form that we completed was, "Would you be willing to rent to 'colored?'" Our answer was "yes," and of course, the first person who inquired was "colored."

Naïvely, I asked few questions of Bill Williams, who was tall and handsome. He and his wife Pauline were Jamaican. Bill spoke in that pleasant, cottony Jamaican accent as he explained that she was in New York, waiting to join him when they could find quarters. It didn't occur to me to lay down any rules or ask for references or agreements, so we were lucky that it turned out to be a fine experience. While we had no TV, they had a large one, which they insisted on putting it in the den even though I assured them they were welcome to have it in their room. We had a washing machine that we shared with them, and they used our coffee pot, creating a mutually supportive relationship.

We invited Bill and Pauline to attend our church and assured them the congregation would welcome them. They were Episcopalians and wanted to attend church in town for a while before coming to our services. Once they began attending our worship, Gordon tried to enlist them. Bill had a beautiful bass voice and Pauline sang alto. Again, they said that they would prefer to wait until the congregation was accustomed to seeing them in the pews. They joined, eventually, adding much to the music program and Pauline became a Sunday School teacher. This was a fine experience for us all, especially considering the racial issues of the day. The whole community was enriched.

Bill and Mark were fond of each other. Mark eagerly waited at the window for Bill at 4:30 each afternoon, and Pauline and I also became close. She wanted to become pregnant but hadn't so far, and I was ready to conceive another myself. It happened for both of us about the same time; and at first, she accused me of sympathizing with her, as I was experiencing the same symptoms as she.

Several years later, we visited Bill and Pauline in England where they were stationed.

Thomas had one more year in a three-year seminary course. He drove to Boston on Tuesday mornings and returned home on Thursday nights to prepare the weekend church program.

I kept things going during the week and also played the organ for services, printed the church bulletin late on Saturday night, and prepared the bread and grape juice for communion. It was easier for Thomas to have me do these things than to enlist some member of the congregation. It was hard for me to meet his demands and care for a baby.

Besides the church work on weekends, I typed, edited, revised, and retyped Thomas's papers on a portable typewriter.

When I heard him lead a couple in their wedding vows—"to love and to cherish"—I was keenly aware of an incongruity. He could elicit the promise from others, but I did not feel cherished by him myself.

We served this community for two years before we began hearing what seemed like petty complaints, and Thomas decided that we should move on. It could have been worked out since they didn't want us to leave, and I didn't want to leave; but he had made up his mind.

We packed and moved, and I unpacked and proceeded to make a new "playhouse." It was the second of 13 moves that we made over the next 24 years; and with each departure, I left part of my heart behind. I began to see a pattern—for him, it was easier to leave than to work out the problem.

Our next assignment was to a church in Enfield, New Hampshire, a greater distance from Boston and a longer commute for Thomas. This was Shaker country, quite hilly and equally beautiful in summer and winter. Photographs of Enfield's Shaker Bridge can be seen in travel magazines. There was good skiing in the northern part of the state, but we didn't have time for winter sports.

In fact, we rarely played at all because of Thomas's academic work. He had completed his basic seminary degree and was now working on a master's in Social Ethics at Boston University School of Theology. Again, he would commute, leaving early Tuesday and returning on Thursday night.

I was without a car during these days but managed quite nicely. We had deep snow many months of the year, and there were other people with whom I could get a ride if necessary. I remember being excited about a trip to the grocery store.

Celebration!

Some of the church members had treated the previous pastor with some nastiness, so that particular element behaved more pleasantly this time, probably in an effort to restore their reputations. Some of our favorites were dear old people who accepted us as family and were patient with our idealism. Among these was one older, unmarried woman named Susie who was anything but "old-maidish." She was supportive of many of Thomas's creative, sometimes outlandish ideas.

We made some close friends in Enfield. There was one couple, Fran and Win, who were childless and often talked about their longing for a baby. They often "boy sat" with Mark and Paul while we made pastoral calls, and sometimes took me with them shopping. An old couple, Joe and Ree, who lived across the street, were not church members but loved Mark and Paul. They looked after them occasionally when I had to be away for a short time and at times took them to their house to play. They filled them with so much candy that I had to insist that they buy some fruit or nuts instead.

My only problem was teaching the boys not to cross the street to their house without someone watching them. Then another problem became evident—Joe and Ree liked to drink. The day I observed Joe watering the light pole with the hose, I decided their "boy sitting" days were over.

We did some meaningful work in Enfield.

Looking back on those early years in the ministry, I began to see two things. One was that the minister's wife was seen by herself, by her husband, and by the culture as an extension of her husband and that the importance of her existence was largely to see to his success. According to my early learning, it was the perfect job description.

The other truth that eventually seeped into my consciousness was the great amount of fear there was in the ministry on the part of the wives as well as the husbands. "Will he be successful?" "Will he get the large, important church?" "Does he have what it takes to compete?" I didn't think much about it at the time because I was too close and too inexperienced to see it.

Each year, at the annual meeting of all the churches in the conference, while the men discussed the problems and solutions of the world, the minister's wives met to determine how we could be of greatest help to our husbands. The Bishop's wife presided over the wives' meeting. On one such occasion, I heard strains of the same theme over and over: "I can't say 'no' to my husband, no matter what else I have to do...I'm tired, but that doesn't seem to matter...What matters is his success." I later remarked to the Bishop's wife, "I think we need to have a meeting of the ministers' wives' husbands." She didn't get it.

Paul was born in September 1957 at nearby Hanover, New Hampshire, the home of Dartmouth College, at Mary Hitchcock Memorial Hospital. It was an easy birth. He was long and healthy, with fingers so long that we thought he might grow up to be an organist. On the third day, he began to show signs of jaundice and required close watching. We were told that possibly there was a problem with his blood, similar to that which occurs in the case of RH-negative babies. While neither of us was RH negative, our blood types were incompatible. Because antibodies left from my previous pregnancy were destroying his hemoglobin, he could die or at least be left brain-damaged.

At the age of five days, Paul had a complete blood exchange transfusion, a risky procedure that was especially hard on his little heart. It took all day, one drop at a time. The operating room was across the hall from my room, and I could hear him crying, causing my breasts to tingle from wanting to nurse him. They gave him a pacifier and fed him intravenously until I could resume breastfeeding. I was told that one of the interns at the hospital donated his own blood. My precious baby made it through the transfusion without skipping a beat and continues to thrive to this day.

Daniel was born on January 23, 1960, at the same hospital as Paul and had the same doctors. I had minor cramps all day but didn't stop to rest because the baby was not due and I was not quite ready. Fran and Win took me to the nearby town of Lebanon to do some shopping, and then I prepared dinner for the district superintendent and his wife. They were coming for the business meeting that was held for the church each quarter.

During dessert, I announced that I would not be joining them for the meeting—I would be going to the hospital instead! "Don't worry," I promised, "I'll get a ride to the hospital." So off the men went to the meeting, leaving the district superintendent's wife to stay with Mark and Paul.

I began calling for a ride and discovered that almost everyone was at the meeting, and the church had no phone. I finally found a friend at home, but her husband had just left for work. "Let me check with my neighbor," she said and soon called back to report that the neighbor could take us but had to finish milking the cow first.

They came, eventually, and we were on our way, driving the 12 miles over snow and icy roads. Daniel entered the world at about 2:00 A.M., healthy and happy. In the event that he had the same problem with antibodies in the blood as Paul, we had to remain in the hospital for a few extra days. He was fine.

After three years in Enfield, Thomas now had two bachelor's degrees and a master's but wanted to continue working toward his doctorate in theology, a Th.D. We hoped that the work on the master's degree would be applied toward the doctorate. However, in the spring, the seminary notified a disappointed Thomas that he was being dropped from the doctoral program. They didn't believe he would need the doctorate for the mission work we planned to do. They didn't realize that Thomas didn't want the degree for our work in missions. Apparently, he needed it desperately for his self-esteem, and I believe that he never quite got over the rejection.

What happened to Thomas in his childhood? All I know is that his mother was not nurturing, was narcissistic herself, and had never gotten along well with either of her sons. She tried to be the center of attention, even to the point of competing with a newborn baby for center stage.

Thomas remembered little from his childhood but did tell of his mother being closed up in her room much of the time and not getting up to fix the boys' breakfast in the mornings, leaving it to their dad. This seemed to be a deep wound for Thomas. When we visited them, it wouldn't take long for his behavior to revert to that of a child. On one of our visits, his mother insisted that we drive to another part of Minneapolis to see a cousin. Thomas balked while his mother stood her ground. They quarreled the entire way, and when we arrived, my mother-in-law jumped out of the car and ran to the door to tell the cousin that Thomas had not wanted to come. I was chagrined.

I finally declared, "If you can't control your behavior around your mother, we'll just stop coming here!" and he seemed to do better after that.

Many times, Thomas seemed to want me to be the mother he never had. For instance, it was very important to him that I get up and fix his breakfast, even after I had been up with a baby or typing his papers late at night. Sometimes, I would bang my fist on the table and scream at him, "I am not your mother!" Recalling that quality of the relationship many years later, I wrote in my book *Love and Lemon Pie, Recipes for the Body and the Soul*, "If you act as if you are your spouse's mother, he will act as if he is your child; if you act as if you are your spouse's child, she will act as if she is your mother."

Together, we had long planned to become affiliated with the Board of World Missions of the Methodist Church, and now was the time. We didn't usually refer to ourselves as "missionaries" because most people had an outdated image of missionaries. Our concept was to go where we could be of help, share cultures and languages and skills as well as Jesus' teachings, not to "save" or "convert." We thought it arrogant of those former missionaries to go to other countries and inform people they were wrong and going to hell if they did not accept "Jesus Christ as their Lord and Savior."

Much harm has been done by this approach; and when we lived in Southeast Asia, we reaped the bitter fruits of such mentality. As it turned out, we gained much more from that experience than we gave.

We both underwent psychological testing before the mission board accepted us to serve in Malaya. We said goodbye to friends, I packed, and we moved to New Haven, Connecticut, to study Mandarin Chinese full-time for a year. We put the three preschoolers, including five-month-old Daniel, into daycare during the day; we were in class for six hours daily and had a lot of homework.

We lived on the second floor of a three-story building. The first floor was an upholstery shop, and the owner, an elderly woman by the name of Mrs. Gold, lived on the top floor. The thermostat for the whole building was in our apartment and was preset and locked so that we could not regulate it. When I asked Mrs. Gold to turn up the heat, she said, "It's plenty hot up here," and refused.

A hurricane came through in early October and with it, low temperatures and we were cold. I asked Mrs. Gold to turn the heat on, but she refused, claiming that she was not required by law to furnish heat until October 15. "The law is for people who won't do the right thing unless they're made to do it," I declared.

I found a solution nevertheless. We had an ice tray with separate little plastic cups shaped like ice cubes that could be filled with water, set on a base, and put into the freezer. I took two or three of the plastic cups containing the frozen cubes, wrapped them in foil to protect the thermostat, and set them on top of the mechanism to lower the surrounding temperature. This caused the heat to come on, and we were a little warmer.

We were in class with young airmen in U. S. Air Force Intelligence who had been screened twice for language aptitude and were on duty when they were in class. They were training to listen by radio to the mainland Chinese military. They had no family responsibilities, and we were expected to keep up with them.

I wanted to cry on that first day when the teacher, a Chinese woman with a dour face, said, "Please turn in your books to page 10." After that, she read, "Wo mang; wo bu mang. Repeat after me—wo mang, wo bu mang."

We repeated, not knowing what we were saying until, finally, we began to catch on. By the end of the year, we could speak almost fluently and read and write about one hundred of the characters. We had also learned about Chinese history and culture from our teachers who were all Chinese, except one couple who had grown up in China as children of missionaries.

I found the process of "Romanization" interesting. The sound of Chinese characters is translated into words that we who use the Roman alphabet can pronounce. For instance, a Chinese speaker of Mandarin would look at the characters for "I" and "busy" and pronounce them "Wo mang," literally "I busy." Using another dialect, the characters would be the same, but the words would be different.

In earlier times, only the elite could learn to read and write because there were 12,000 or more different characters. Their numbers grew and expanded as the Chinese world enlarged and incorporated words from other languages. For that reason, the written language was mastered only by full-time scholars in the early days.

The Chinese invented Romanization many years ago in order for the masses to be educated. There are various systems, one of which is the Yale system, which we learned. We became acquainted with the Wade-Giles method, also, that was used elsewhere. Since then, a new, universal system called Pinyin has been created for the international press, commerce, and government.

All the Chinese dialects use tones along with enunciation. In Mandarin, there are four tones, and the tone that the speaker

uses determines how the listener will interpret the words. For instance, "ma" said with a falling tone means "scold," while "ma" said with a low tone means "horse." Mother is "ma" with a high level tone, and "ma" with a rising tone makes the statement into a question. Therefore, one must be careful to use the right tone.

Once in a restaurant, I meant to ask for sugar but what the waitress understood was "soup" and answered that they had no soup. It was confusing for a few moments. And in one class session, I stated that I was going to the brothel when I meant to say "hospital." See what I mean? The two words are pronounced the same but have different tones.

It was an especially rough year. We were without any sense of community even though we did socialize with our instructors

The weather was cold and wet, and the children brought home every known childhood disease. I had mumps myself, first in one side, then the other, and had several sinus infections. I stayed home when one of the boys was sick, under the assumption that it was more important for the husband to learn the language than for me since his work was more important than mine.

Now wait! This was an accepted supposition that I bought into as much as anyone else. A lot of my behaviors were based upon false assumptions and unworkable agreements, all childhood learning.

In the meantime, I had a machine that played our lessons from vinyl disks, and this helped me keep up. As soon as the heat in the apartment came on at 5:00 A.M., I got up and had a few minutes to study before time to prepare breakfast and get the children dressed.

Trying to fulfill someone else's goals is a tragic mistake.

CHAPTER SIX

GOING TO THE MISSION FIELD

We were both commissioned as a missionary team by Thomas's Bishop in a formal service in Mankato, Minnesota, at Christmas, 1960.

In the summer of 1961, it was time to visit family one last time and say goodbye before sailing for Southeast Asia, where we had been assigned to serve in a small town on the Malay Peninsula. We would disembark in Singapore. We spent a few days with my parents in Georgia and Thomas's parents met us in New York to see us off. We underwent physicals, interviews, shots, and briefing at the office of the Board of World Missions and made all the other necessary preparations. I took the boys to the World's Fair one day, while Thomas took our barrels and crates to the warehouse to be shipped separately.

We departed New York on the *Queen Elizabeth* and landed in Southampton, England, five days later. We enjoyed being on the deck, basking in the sun those warm days on the ocean, with the weather growing cooler and damper as we neared England. Fog hung over the surface of the ocean in the early mornings, reminding me of fields of snow in New England or, if flying in an airplane, looking down on a cloudy sky from above.

We went by train to Bury St. Edmonds to visit our old friends Bill and Pauline Williams, who had lived with us in Maine. They had three children by this time. We learned that St. Edmonds was buried there—all except his head—which was never found. He was a king who was martyred for some reason.

The weather was cold and damp in August and at night, I put my feet into the sleeves of Thomas's sweater to keep them warm. It was wonderful to see our old friends again. We boarded another ship, a converted cargo carrier, which was charming and comfortable but lacking one important thing—laundry service. I washed our things by hand and found places to hang them to dry. Otherwise, the service and accommodations were first-class and included a supervised program for the children.

The children ate dinner at 5:30, then we went to our cabin to get them bathed and dressed for bed. When they were settled, we returned to a separate dining room for a four-course meal while the steward looked after the boys. I still had some of my pretty dresses from the Miss Georgia pageant that I hadn't had much opportunity to wear, so it was fun to get into them again. We met some nice people on the voyage to Singapore, including the people assigned to our table and a young mother who was traveling with her two sons to meet her husband in Kuala Lumpur, where they were to live. We visited them after arriving in Malaya, and their boys came to see us.

On a Sunday morning, near the end of our five-week trip, we disembarked for the day at Penang, an island off the west coast of the Malay Peninsula. It was absolutely beautiful, with modern, white buildings and brilliantly colored flowers and trees. We attended a service at the Methodist Church there, led by an American missionary. I read an announcement in the bulletin about a curry supper that was being held to raise money to buy new hymnals and was struck by the thought that, perhaps, we are too prone to impose our own Western customs and culture in other lands. We sailed the next morning, September 14, 1961, to Singapore, our destination. How excited we were! In our first official letter back home, we wrote:

We are looking into a kaleidoscope—complex, multicolored, and presenting a different and exciting picture each time we turn it to look from a different angle. Chinese, Indians, Pakistanis, Europeans, Eurasians, Indonesians, Malays, and Aborigines live and work side by side in relative harmony. To a great extent, each group maintains its own customs, language, and religious practices. Christianity, Buddhism, Hinduism,

Confucianism, Taoism, Sikhism, various spirit-religions, and ancestor worship have a major influence upon Malayan life. Yet, most consider themselves Malayans; and in addition to the language of their racial group, most people speak Malay, the national language.

We visit dimly lit Malay homes, sit upon the floor, eating with our fingers, and communicate in Malay. Again, we are invited to dine with Indian friends who speak Tamil, some Malay, and English, perhaps. This time we sit upon chairs before a table and eat with our fingers from a banana leaf. When we go Chinese, we eat with chopsticks and do our best with Mandarin, the dialect we studied at Yale.

Representatives from the head office were there to meet and welcome us. We spent a few days visiting headquarters and meeting local officials and missionaries. Then we boarded an overnight train for Kuala Lumpur, the capital of The Federation of Malaya. I had ridden trains before, but this was the first time I had made the trip in a sleeper, so I felt very special.

I couldn't understand why Thomas was in an especially grumpy mood at this point, embarking on an adventure few people are privileged to have. Then I remembered. He had expressed disappointment in having been assigned to such an unimportant outpost. He had insisted on being appointed to serve in Hong Kong, the gateway into China and where he felt the "real" action was. Yet, it would have meant having to learn Cantonese, the dialect spoken there.

From Kuala Lumpur, we went the 80 winding and breathtakingly gorgeous miles by car to our assignment, the small town of Raub, in the mountains and rain forests in the state of Pahang. The peninsula was not developed from the middle of the country to the east coast, but it was all considered east so that, even though Raub was right in the middle of the peninsula, it was still called "East Coast." Young adults dreaded being assigned there as teachers, doctors, or civil servants because of its remoteness.

Celebration!

Mable Mitchell, a missionary and the principal of the Methodist Girls' School in Raub, sent her driver to fetch us. I marveled at the beautiful scenery as we snaked our way into the mountains —palm trees of all kinds, tree ferns, orchids, red "fire" trees. I looked over my left shoulder as the afternoon slipped toward evening and saw mist rising through the thick foliage. I practiced my Mandarin with the driver, a Chinese man called Ah Tec, who knew little English but with whom we became warmly acquainted by the time we reached our destination.

"Mitchie" had seen to it that the house was clean and furnished with fresh linens and was waiting to greet us and served us a nice supper. I was anxious to see my house, especially the kitchen. The night before we sailed from New York, I watched a movie on TV about Malaya in which the starring character was an aggressive cobra. I entered the darkened house now, found the light switch, and made my way to the kitchen. As I opened a long, narrow cabinet, I thought of the cobra in that movie. Suddenly, out jumped—a lizard!

The house had possibilities. It was simple but comfortable, with bare, concrete floors that were painted red and stained the bottoms of our feet. The whitewash on the walls was peeling and moldy from the humidity. The simple furniture was Norwegian modern, in pretty good shape, and the outside was stucco over concrete blocks. There was no hot water, but thank goodness, there was indoor plumbing. I didn't want to return to the experience of my childhood and be without that convenience. The three bedrooms, a bath, and a servant's room with bath opened out onto an atrium in the middle of the house that provided good ventilation and was a great place for houseplants. I observed that in this part of the world, kitchens, unlike those in the U. S., were not planned with conveniences in mind, and people were not familiar with the notion of having a certain place for things and putting them there.

The house sat on a high hill overlooking the Methodist Girls' School and *padang* (playing field) below. We were on the edge of town and not far from the jungle, where we were told tigers roamed. Neighbors said they could hear them, but we didn't worry.

I was glad that I had packed a trunk with necessities to bring with us on the ship—five sets of sheets, five plates, five sets of tableware, five towels, etc., for our belongings didn't arrive until November. This helped us get along until the rest came.

Ah Tec, his wife Ah Tai, and their three sons lived a stone's throw from us down the hill. Ah Tai and I became good friends. She taught me to cook Chinese food and Malayan curry as well as how to cook rice so that the grains didn't stick together, no matter how big a crowd I was preparing for. We spoke in Mandarin only since Ah Tai knew little English. Their boys were each just a year older than ours, and they became close friends and playmates. Ah Tec was Mitchie's driver and otherwise helped around the school, and Ah Tai was her cook and housekeeper.

One of the schoolteachers came that first morning to assist me in getting settled. She led me to a store formerly patronized by some Australians who had operated a gold mine outside of town, assuming that's what I would prefer. I found only expensive, imported canned food—catsup, spam, canned vegetables, bread, eggs, and a few other things, for a start. I was alarmed, wondering how I would feed the family on these products and at these prices.

I ventured out on my own the next day and found the market, where I bought wonderful fresh fruits and vegetables in addition to fish and shrimp caught that morning in the ocean and trucked in. I discovered the bakery, where I often stopped for freshly baked bread, sometimes enjoying the pleasant aroma while I waited for it to come out of the oven. Few of the vendors at the market spoke English, so I got along with Mandarin and, in time, learned enough Malay to get by.

I had to learn to cook all over again, making substitutions for products that I couldn't buy. I modified some of the local products or learned to cook them according to Asian custom. The sugar was so coarse that it had to be dissolved in water; the flour was coarse, too, and the salt not as salty. Jello wouldn't jell, puddings wouldn't thicken, and some baked goods wouldn't rise.

I abandoned the idea of using local beef, which was not aged and not butchered according to specific cuts. I once determined to make hamburgers, purchased a meat grinder and went to the market for a pound of beef. With a large knife, the vender swatted some flies off the cow hanging there and whacked off a piece of flesh. I washed it thoroughly, put it through the grinder several times to get out the gristle and proceeded to cook patties. The taste cannot be described and eating it was like chewing leather.

Chickens were allowed to run free and were tough and stringy. I discovered that Mr. Ling, the merchant I had visited that first day, could order frozen steaks and chicken from the States, which we ate on special occasions. It was cheaper and certainly tastier than the local variety.

We had been warned that we might experience culture shock, the trauma of going from our culture to one less developed and drastically different. The odor in town was the one aspect that took some getting used to. There was no real sewage system. Most waste—urine, trash, and garbage—went into drains, cement ditches along the streets with no curbs. In addition, the storekeepers spread garlic, onions, and fish on the sidewalk in front of their shops to dry in the sun. For a while, the stench caused an ache across my forehead; but the pain mysteriously disappeared after a couple of weeks!

Learning to drive on the "wrong" side of the street was a challenge, too, and we had to be careful to avoid ending up in a drain. We settled in quite easily otherwise.

I learned to make curry, which called for a special combination of spices from the market. I told the woman vendor whether I planned to use chicken or beef, and she made up a mixture accordingly, dampened it, and wrapped it in a palm leaf and tied it with a dried vine. I also purchased freshly grated coconut for the curry, making coconut milk by pouring hot water through it. The inside of the coconut was soft, unlike that which we buy in the U. S. I continued to buy staples from Mr. Ling. If I bought a *kati* of rice—a little more than a pound—he formed a cone from newspaper, put the rice in, folded it over, and tied it with a vine, leaving a loop for hanging the package on my bicycle handlebars. When I shopped at his store, he insisted that I sit down, have a soft drink, and visit while he collected the items on my list. How nurturing it was to sit and be accommodated in this way.

Mark started first grade at the government's "Mamoud School for Boys" in January and got along well as the only non-Asian in the school. We were concerned that he be treated fairly, neither special nor discriminated against. I believe that this was true for the most part. Mark often complained about one of the men teachers who seemed to hassle him for no reason, though he was known as the best-behaved child in the whole school. He also was distressed by one teacher's practice of hitting any student with a cane who did not answer correctly. I wept the day Mark came home and said, "Mama, not one single person had to hit me today!" I certainly had a talk with the headmaster who appeared to be an enlightened person. He listened carefully.

Besides the Methodist Girls' School and the Mamoud School for Boys, which were free, there were private Chinese, Malay, and Hindu schools for children whose parents wanted them to maintain their own traditional culture, religion, and language. They still had to learn English and National Language, which was required at all schools.

Ready-made clothes and shoes were not available, so I had them made to fit. Among the clothes I had made for myself were a *sam foo*, the dress with the high, mandarin collar and a tight skirt with splits up the sides—pretty sexy—and a *chiang sam*, a pajama-like, two-piece outfit. I wore the *chiang sam* and

Celebration!

a straw hat to market on my bicycle sometimes, waving at everyone along the way and feeling like Katherine Hepburn herself. Asian women wore their clothes more tightly fitting than we "Europeans," so I had to request a little more room in mine. I had a Malay outfit made with the *sarong* (skirt) and a *kabaya* (blouse) embroidered with Malaysian silver. I purchased a pink silk sari embroidered with silver and had a matching blouse made. After we returned to the States, I presented programs with slides and had local women model the three costumes. When I remarried, years later, I made my wedding dress out of that pink sari. That story will have to wait.

Stores were open seven days a week, and I occasionally had my hair cut or permed on a Sunday afternoon. The fascinating method of shampooing reminded me of Mama making biscuits back on the farm in Georgia. The operator splashed a bit of water on the top of my head, then added some shampoo and kneaded. She added water and kneaded, added more water and kneaded, until my entire head was lathered. Next, we went behind the building, where I bent over while she rinsed my head with the water hose. At least, they had dryers. In spite of the primitive methods, my hair always turned out great.

I painted the living and dining areas and the kitchen a gentle blue, made a yellow skirt for the sink and had an island made for the kitchen and some screens for the windows. Mosquitoes were abundant. I paid for most of this with money from the committee that controlled expenditures for the mission.

The floor was hopeless. Ah Tec and I put together a rattan mat for the living area since there was nothing more that I could do with the floor. The windows were louvered and not conducive to curtains, so I made yellow ruffles to frame the windows, creating a pretty effect.

There were orchids and red and yellow hibiscus in the yard and by the kitchen door, a banana tree that provided a steady supply of tree-ripened fruit. A friend brought avocadoes when he came to town. It took a while to get accustomed to the less-flavorful fruit from our stores here after we returned to the States.

I hired a gardener to help improve the yard and rehabilitate the flowers and grass. He had been watering and cutting the grass while the house was vacant, but now it needed more attention. I ordered some compost but discovered that I had to supervise its application because he subscribed to the belief that if a little was helpful, a whole lot would be even better. He spoke his Tamil dialect and Malay only, and I had not yet learned much Malay.

Our first servant was a young Chinese woman who knew more Malay and English than Mandarin, so we agreed to communicate in English and that she would assist me in working with the gardener. I soon needed her assistance in speaking with him and called to her, "Mae Ying, please come. I need my interpreter."

She came out, looking very puzzled, until her face lit up with understanding. "Oh, I washed it this morning!" she proudly announced. I never figured out what she thought an interpreter was.

Esa was our next *amah* (nanny/servant), who assisted with the cooking and housework and helped to look after Daniel. She loved him as her own, and he was quite attached to her, too.

Raub was a small town, not including the "new village" down the road and people who lived in rural areas. The "new villages" were established during the long struggle with the communist insurgents called "The Emergency." It ended in 1959 and was much like our experience in Vietnam except that, in this case, the British were successful. The guerillas leeched off the people who lived in the jungle and confiscated food and medicine, so the British moved everyone from remote areas into protected "new villages," starving the insurgents out.

Two routes led from Raub to the new village near us, one of which passed the Christian cemetery. The villagers declared they could hear the ghosts speaking English there, so they took the other way.

Celebration!

The country has three predominant ethnic groups, Chinese, Malay, and Indian—Punjabis from northern India and Tamils from the south. All others, including ourselves, were considered European. We enjoyed all the various kinds of food, and our boys did as well. Everyone knew who we were and were delightfully friendly. Malaya is a Muslim country but recognizes all religions and designates holidays for each one. Malays are required to be Muslim though, so we were prohibited by law from proselytizing among them. It was not our style anyway, even though we strongly pushed religious freedom for everyone.

We enjoyed eating at several outdoor cafes. When we were still fairly new to town, we ate with the boys' school principal, Mr. Ung, at such a place. I noticed a man sitting in the corner, watching us and appearing to be waiting for something. I learned from the waiter that the man was a beggar, not asking for money, only waiting for us to finish, so he could eat the leavings.

"Here, let us buy him a meal," I said.

"That's not a good idea. If you do that, you'll start a precedent, and he'll never leave you alone," the waiter explained. We tried to respect the local customs and to avoid interfering, so we simply made sure we left enough food for the man to have an adequate meal.

The boys' favorite treats were corn ice cream and another popular dish, ice *kachang*, which was a combination of cubes of gelatin, mixed with ice cream, corn, and kidney beans.

Chinese New Year was similar to our Christmas, New Year's, Easter, Fourth of July, Halloween, and Thanksgiving all rolled into one and lasted a week. Many of the town folks, especially our church members, neighbors, and the merchants whom we patronized, invited us. We started early in the morning making our calls, discovering that no matter what hour it was, we were expected to eat a full meal. At bedtime, we dragged our sated bodies home.

One very old tradition associated with this occasion is that, no matter how poor the family is, they must have good food, and they must do something to fix up the house if it means only painting the front door.

Another old custom, which is surely not strictly observed, is about making a fresh start financially. One must pay any outstanding debts if one is able; if not, the debtee must forgive the unpaid obligations.

We twice observed a very interesting occasion that was the most important Hindu religious observance—Thiapusam. Participants prepared for the celebration by cleansing themselves through prayer and fasting. They shaved their heads on the day of the festival, pierced their backs, cheeks and tongues with hooks, put skewers through their tongues and cheeks, and walked on hot coals. Some carried large frames on their shoulders that held steel needles which punctured the back and chest. Some walked on hot coals and flagellated themselves in hopes that all transgressions would be forgiven by the gods, that the devotee would be cured of disease, or that the person would have better luck generally in the coming year. Perhaps a couple had not been able to conceive, or they wished for good crops or a better financial situation. It was claimed that the devotees were able to go into a trance, felt no pain, and did not bleed or scar.

At the end of the long day, the whole assembly carried torches and beat drums as they paraded through the town, pulling along an elegant, magnificently lighted carriage with an idol inside. The observance took place once on a Sunday evening during our church service. We had quite a competition, with the Hindu temple right next door. On one of these occasions, we ran into a Hindu friend who gave us helpful information about the ritual. We ended up at one of the outdoor food shops and had a delightful conversation about religion in general.

As a Muslim, Esa did not eat or touch pork. During the month-long observance of Ramadan, she did not even swallow her saliva or brush her teeth from 7:00 A.M. to 7:00 P.M. I was impressed that she was willing to wear rubber gloves when preparing any food for us that included pork. After moving to Singapore, we were astonished to hear that she was arrested and jailed for being in the car with a man to whom she was not married.

We observed a Punjabi Sikh funeral one day, right down the hill from our house. The body was placed on a scaffold with camphor wood underneath to minimize the odor of the burning flesh, and the whole thing was set afire. Punjabi people are originally from northern India and warlike, but the ones in this country were peaceful and loyal to Malaya.

There was an outbreak of cholera once not far from us, and we had to have shots. They were not given routinely like others because they would last only six months. The best plan was to be inoculated when there was an outbreak in the vicinity. During the night after getting the shot, I suffered all the symptoms of the disease, including cramps and nausea. Our doctor friend came to the house during the night, determined that it was probably a stomach "bug" caused by something I had eaten, not cholera, and gave me an injection. By the next morning, I was fine.

We concluded, finally, that my discomfort was from the meal we had eaten at the outdoor café the previous evening. I remembered reaching with my chopsticks into a small bowl containing hot peppers in vinegar, which had been sitting out for several hours. Perhaps a fly had contaminated the peppers during its visit to the table. Checking with the others who had been in the party, I learned I was the only one who had eaten the peppers and the only one who got sick.

Mark always appreciated the female gender; and at the age of six, fell in love with a little Chinese girl, Susie, who was his age and lived in town and liked him in return. He always looked for her when we went to the store or out to eat, his eyes lighting up like a neon sign when he saw her. We teased him in a good-natured way but not enough to embarrass him. He also made good friends at school and rode his bicycle around the neighborhood to visit them.

Paul, who was about four years old at the time, spent his days playing, learning to whistle, making paper airplanes and boats, and exploring the territory. He was quite independent and self-sufficient, dressing and otherwise taking care of himself. Sometimes, he came out with the most hilarious remarks, and it was amusing to hear him talk Pidgin English with the local children.

He was performing some circus tricks on a tree limb one day when he fell and broke his arm. Peter, Ah Tec, and Ah Tai's oldest son, who was seven or eight years old, brought him to the house and from there we took him to the local hospital. The doctor, a Tamil Indian who was a member of our church, anesthetized Paul and reset his arm, leaving the cast for the orderly to finish. In about a week, the cast softened, so I took Paul back to the hospital, where they removed the cast, revealing a big lump at the site of the break. "No problem," they said and put on a new cast.

I was so worried that the arm wouldn't be right that I called an American doctor friend who worked in a clinic on the coast and consulted him. He reassured me that the arm would be all right and, sure enough, when the final cast was removed, the arm was fine.

Sweet and adorable Daniel was into everything. There was not a cupboard or drawer he couldn't open. He was late talking and late being potty trained and, in fact, was slow in everything. When he wet the floor, he brought a rag and wiped up the puddle. He organized people and things into categories. All food was cake, all animals were dogs and all young men were Dons, in reference to a good friend named Don, a short-term missionary who spent a lot of time at our house. We had not yet realized that Dan had some brain damage.

Mark had a series of tonsil infections, so I took him to the hospital in nearby Kuala Lipis where there was a Medico team made up of American doctors and nurses, and they performed his tonsillectomy. I had planned to stay until Mark was discharged, but the doctor insisted that I go home, maintaining that Mark would be better off without me. I complied but deeply regretted it after Mark later said to me, accusingly, "You left me." I have apologized to him more than once.

Yet, I think the Medico team spoiled him a bit.

We had a lot of company, people from other locations who liked coming to Pahang where it was scenic and cool. I planned and prepared food ahead of time when we had a family or group of people coming, so that I could be free to show them interesting sites and escort them to meet people in our community.

The bishop of Minnesota, Otto Nall, and his wife Frances came for a few days as did the new field secretary from New York. Dr. Olin Stockwell, head of the theological college in Singapore, his wife Esther, and Thomas's parents from Minnesota came also.

Thomas drove the Nalls down the mountain to Kuala Lumpur at the end of their visit to catch their plane. They left a little late, and they were going too fast as they made their way around the mountainous curves when a 14-foot iguana darted from the jungle on their left side and ran in front of the car. Before Thomas could slow down, both axles had bumped over it—thump, thump, jarring the passengers considerably. As they looked back, they saw the reptile dragging itself across the road and down the other side.

The bishop later wrote that, for years, he had not been able to hear with his left ear in spite of visits to several specialists. Apparently, a tube had closed and could not be opened in any way.

"But the day we rode over that iguana, my ear opened up, and I have been able to hear perfectly ever since," he wrote. "Thanks for the Miracle of the Iguana!"

Take a risk, get outside your comfort zone,
and explore your world.
That's where all the "goodies" are.

CHAPTER SEVEN

LIFE AND WORK IN RAUB, MALAYA

Until the 20th century, Malaya did not educate its girls, so there were no schools for them until the Methodists came and began to establish them in the late 1800s. They eventually set up boys' and girls' schools all over the peninsula and Singapore. The schools were built and maintained by missions but regulated by the central government, and the teachers were paid by the government. I'm sure the church has turned over those schools entirely to the government by now.

English was the teaching medium in Malaya, thanks to the British, and was the language used for government and business transactions. Everyone who had ever been to school spoke English; but students also studied Malay or, as it were later called, National Language. Malay was the vernacular and was spoken by most Malayans except the higher government officials and educated people who could speak the more elite form, similar to Indonesian.

I ordered a home-study course for Mark to supplement his school work, and we worked mostly on reading and phonics since that was more my strength than math. Today, Mark attributes the fact that he is a good speller to those times when I taught him at home.

Paul learned to speak Malay from the gardener while Mark studied National Language at school. As the sense of nationalism grew, we were all encouraged to learn National Language, even those who had grown up speaking Malay. Thomas and I signed up for the training, but when we saw that everyone in the class already knew Malay, we dropped out. I still had to learn enough to deal with hired household help and vendors.

Celebration!

We served a small church in town and were later assigned to another congregation in Kuala Lipis, in addition, about 35 miles north through the mountains. We helped train ministerial students Samuel Wong, Richard Liew, and Loh Sin Tech who came from the theological college in Singapore for six months at a time on internships. Thomas met with the intern for an hour in the morning, working on sermon preparation and delivery, using our tape recorder. We greatly enjoyed the fellowship with these young men.

We worked with the Methodist Girls' School as well, where I taught scripture before and after classes. Other work included planning and conducting church activities, making pastoral calls, and working with the Sunday School. We set up Raub's first Vacation Church School, Religious Emphasis Week for the girls' school, and programs for the high school youth group and the young adult group.

Thomas served on some of the conference boards and provided workshops all over the peninsula in pastoral care, worship, and how to conduct community surveys. He took Mark and Paul with him on these trips if they were on school break.

In addition to our work in Raub and Kuala Lipis, we managed the mission bungalow at a beautiful mountain resort called Fraser's Hill, about an hour away. We were assigned the job because we were the closest of all the mission stations. The English-style village included cottages for government personnel and church and business groups as well as private owners. Our facility was available to all missionaries in Southeast Asia for study and rest.

Vegetables that couldn't be grown below thrived in the cooler climate of the mountain, and we could buy fresh whole milk and some other products not available in Raub.

We went once a month to arrange for maintenance and to pay the help. We also booked the guests and kept the books. We took the whole family sometimes and stayed three or four days. We could request certain menus, and the food was always delicious. The weather was cool on the mountain, so we enjoyed the fireplace, especially during the monsoon seasons.

During our time in Raub, we hosted a ten-man caravan of students who were on spring break from the theological college in Singapore. Thomas organized and trained them before they made the rounds. Equipped with splendid singing voices, three and four languages and dialects each, and deep personal commitments, they went from house to house and from shop to shop, speaking to people about Jesus, with great response. They were not turned away from even one door. The college later sent a group of interns to serve in a group ministry under Thomas's supervision. They made Raub their headquarters but lived and worked with Tamil people at the rubber estates, who seemed very eager to hear the gospel. Thomas received many kudos from the college for his work with the students.

Another time, we were hosts to a fine choir that came from a church in Kuala Lumpur. We rented the new town hall and had a big, appreciative crowd. Thomas arranged for the concert, and I organized housing within our church community.

Until I reread some of the letters I had sent home, I had forgotten how frustrated and angry we became over the patterns established by the 19th-century style of missionaries. The earlier missionaries were paternalistic and controlling and created helpless, dependent people of those they had been sent to serve. While they had money to distribute as they wished, we, the new missionaries, had no control over the considerable funds that came through in our name from individuals and supporting churches.

Our constituents in Raub could not understand that we weren't rich and that we couldn't give money to their favorite projects, and were often resentful. A young person would call and say, "Would you have the Reverend come and pick us up for the meeting?" We knew the car was a barrier, as it represented a financial inequality and imbalance of power in the eyes of our church community. We wished we could simply turn it in and ride bicycles, but that was not feasible.

The day had come when the missionaries needed to step down from positions of leadership and do more to train local people. We were looking forward to the day when missionaries would not be pastoring churches but would have trained self-governing, self-sufficient, indigenous people to do so, with us in the background. A good example of this was a conversation between Thomas and one of our interns, Sam Wong.

Sam said, "Thomas, I wish that on your next tour of duty here, you would be a missionary to the aboriginals and that I could be your assistant."

Thomas, whose language aptitude was not as good as Sam's, replied, "No, Sam. You would be the missionary, and I would be your assistant."

We were dismayed when the pastor of the Methodist Tamil congregation, Rev. Ratnasami, sought Thomas's advice regarding his work, as if we knew better than he.

One of my issues was the Asian custom of taking on a Western name once they became Christian, and I often suggested that they keep their Chinese or Indian name even after converting. Brides usually wore Western-style wedding dresses, white veil and all, while I thought their own native costumes were more beautiful. I disliked seeing Christianity associated with the Western culture.

We followed the Cuban crisis with great concern, and all the civil rights activities especially.

We were embarrassed over the negative news from the United States about our nation's racial troubles. The tragic events in Mississippi were transpiring about that time, and we were heartsick when people asked us, "Why do Americans hate people with dark skin?" We did our best to explain that this was not true of most Americans, that we certainly did not agree with it, and that many white people were working toward greater justice and understanding. The mission board expected us to send newsletters every quarter to our supporting churches and individual sponsors, and we sent the same letters to our friends and relatives, mentioning the issues that affected our work. This excerpt is from one such letter.

"We believe America is fortunate to have the right kind of people leading the social revolution that is taking place. Martin Luther King is a Christian man who believes in peaceful change and if the Negro does not follow his leading, he may follow the Black Muslims or other less desirable revolutionaries. Other nations that have had revolutions have not been as fortunate as we."

I learned later that this part of my letter alienated Mama's family and a lot of people in our supporting churches in the South, including my own home church.

Many of the members of our church in Raub were young adults, mostly teachers and civil servants, for whom we had an active program and to whom we became very close. One of the frustrations was that after being assigned to Raub, those from more developed parts of the country transferred back home at the first opportunity and those who had grown up in Raub were eager to get to more exciting locations. So there was much fluctuation in our constituency.

We had an active youth group, and while many were not Christians, they liked attending our activities. Some of them were Hindu, but most were either Christians or Buddhists. Most of these religions allowed other gods, and their families didn't mind if they attended Christian functions but didn't want them to reject their own religion or to be baptized. Some of the Chinese parents believed that people of different religions go to different heavens and didn't want their children to be separated in the afterlife by becoming Christian. One of our church members was a Chinese high school boy whose Buddhist father was a school principal. The father required his son to bow to him as a traditional sign of respect; but the boy, being a Christian and more modern than his father, refused. It caused a deep rift between them. We often observed that these young people were living between two cultures—one that was dying and one that was struggling to be born.

Our house was a popular place for young people to meet, whether it was a church activity or not. Sometimes a committee of high school students met at our house, perhaps because it was not as crowded as theirs, was quieter, and also had a small refrigerator that made ice. The members of the church youth group often used our kitchen to make refreshments for their meetings, and it was not uncommon at the end of the term for three or four students to come to our house to study for their Senior Cambridge exams, spending the night on the floor in their bedrolls. We were astonished at how much the young people knew about our culture, our songs and movies, and the popular culture in general, along with many misconceptions.

The Asian people did not appear to have the same need for privacy as we did. Knocking before entering another's house was not expected—they just walked in. In Kuala Lumpur or Singapore, if a university student met a friend who needed a place to stay for a while, the family said, "Sure, no problem," and no matter how many people were already in residence, they simply put a folding cot in the corner of the living or dining room.

We took several carloads of our young adults to a conference in Singapore one Friday night, a long drive, and the same young teacher who had accompanied me to the store that first day rode in our car. When we came to a town and it was time for a stop, I informed Ching Lee that I needed to go to the bathroom. There were no service stations along these roads. Ching Lee said, "Come with me," and we entered a little store along the street, continuing into the family quarters in the back where there were several people sitting around a table, eating. Ching Lee parted the curtain and, without missing a step, announced that we were going to use their facility. They nodded, and we proceeded, thanking them as we left. I assumed that my companion knew these people, but I was wrong; we were travelers, just passing through.

It was not uncommon for a guest, without asking, to bring along another guest that we hadn't invited; in such a case, we simply put on some more rice and made enough for all. It also was not uncommon for an invited guest to fail to show up for dinner because for them, it was more of a loss of face to say "no" outright than to not keep the commitment.

We went on a unique outing one day—a rafting excursion—with the young adult group consisting mostly of teachers and civil servants. We drove into a remote area and stopped along a river where the men in our group chopped down some heavy bamboo poles for the raft. They tied them together and put a floatation device underneath. When the raft was finished, we all climbed aboard with our food and drinks and pushed off. It was soon apparent that we were overloaded, as the conveyance sank about two inches beneath the surface. We stayed afloat though, paddling, squealing, and laughing our way down the river while curious aboriginals peered at us from the jungle.

A couple with whom we were friendly operated and lived on a rubber plantation. They had us to dinner on occasion, sometimes when there were other interesting visitors. The wife was Malay, and the husband was an Englishman who had lived in Malaya many years. They had no children but had a pair of gibbons who were quite entertaining and mischievous. If you were the least bit careless, you could lose your car keys, false teeth, glasses, or other articles that they liked to collect and hide. We enjoyed several exotic meals at their house.

The Sultan of Pahang, who was equivalent to a governor, made a practice of visiting all the towns in the state once a year. We attended the festivities celebrating his arrival—a dinner, music, and dancing. On this occasion, he also dedicated the new town hall.

After the dinner, many people sat against the wall watching the dancing. Mitchie whispered to me, "The sultan will probably

ask you to dance." We left right away because I didn't know the dances, but later I wished that we had stayed. I still can't believe that I passed up a great opportunity. Why, I could be writing at this very minute that I danced with the Sultan of Pahang!

The sultan, as a Muslim, was allowed to have only four wives at once, but could trade one or more for a newer or better model at any time. His position was hereditary. I also learned that if he had discovered that we had lived there more than six months, he wouldn't have spoken to us in English but in Malay.

Mark, Paul, and I went with Thomas to a nearby town where he was to speak to a Methodist youth group. We expected to visit some friends while there, but another friend had been invited to a Malay wedding and insisted that we attend with her. Off we went after being assured that it would be all right. The ceremony was held at a club, the men seated in chairs on the outside and the women on the inside.

I sat next to two lovely young Malay women who were dressed in beautiful Malay costumes embroidered with gold and silver threads. I talked with them for quite a while and apologized for not being dressed suitably. One of them said my dress was just fine, and the other said, "Oh, a beautiful girl like you does not need beautiful clothes. You see, we are so ugly that we have to have beautiful dresses to make up for it!" I remarked that I thought that was an extremely dear thing to say, and we three had a good laugh.

The couple arrived very unceremoniously after about half an hour, to the accompaniment of some loud and garish music. They climbed up to an elaborately decorated platform, each escorted by an attendant. They sat for 10 minutes with very serious facial expressions and downcast eyes. The priest came in about half an hour after this, wearing a white cloth headpiece to denote that he had been to Mecca. He mumbled a few words of Malay into the mike and walked away, wiping his brow. The couple sat for 10 more minutes and then it was over, except for a delicious curry dinner. By now, we had learned to eat delicately with our fingers as was the local custom, using the right hand only and making sure to avoid getting food above the second knuckle. When the feast was over, we were each given a basket with an egg in it, a symbol of fertility, I'm sure.

We observed the process of rubber tapping. The tappers arrived at about 4:00 in the morning when the latex was running. They collected it from troughs attached to the tree trunk below a place where a section of the bark had been removed and slits cut in the tree. The pay was good, and the workers could still get in a day's work elsewhere.

We were called upon occasionally to bring our roomy Volkswagen microbus to transport a corpse from the hospital to the home of the deceased, regardless of religion. This was especially common when it was at the wrong time for one to touch a dead body, according to the stars.

We had a death in our church community once, and Thomas couldn't find anyone to make a coffin because the carpenter was building a structure for a wedding. It would bring bad luck to deal with a dead body during that period. Thomas enlisted the young men in the family, and they got the task done quite nicely, digging the grave themselves. There were no funeral parlors or undertakers in this part of the world, obviously. I often noted that life in this land was lived more closely to the earth and more in touch with real life than in our own. Children were not shuttled away at times of birth and death, for example, and they often took an active part in funerals.

The Chinese Buddhist funerals were interesting. The mourners had a parade made up of friends and family members, and if there were not enough participants to make up a respectable crowd, some were hired. They marched through the streets with drums and horns, carrying banners and flags and paper models of fine mansions, jewelry, automobiles, and cash. They set fire to the whole thing at some point, for the purpose of sending these items to heaven with the deceased. Who says you can't take it with you?

Celebration!

There was a family of Tamil Indians who lived across the road from us, all of whom were members of our church except the father, who was somewhat agnostic. There were 13 children, some of whom were grown and working, two who were beautiful young daughters, and some darling little ones. The father, an alcoholic, died from an overdose of some kind of medication that he took while under the influence. Thomas was away, and I was called to the hospital, arriving just as he was taking his last breath and the aides were trying to resuscitate him. Thomas helped arrange the funeral, and I stayed with the wife and children who were surrounded by many friends. The body was brought home and placed on the dining table that was brought into the living room.

The wife approached the corpse after a while, took his hand, and finding that it was stiff, she let out a scream and uttered something in Tamil. At the cemetery, as the coffin was lowered into the grave, each one took a handful of dirt and tossed it in. Back at the house, friends of the wife took her into the back, where they undressed her, doused her with water and dried her off, dressed her in clean clothes, and brushed her hair; then they took buckets of water and washed down all the floors. I thought this was symbolic of a fresh start. All of them, including the non-Christians, expressed deep appreciation for our involvement.

This family belonged to the Mar Thomas Church when they lived in their native India. Legend has it that Thomas, one of Jesus' 12 apostles, traveled to India where he organized a Church. This church later became part of the Methodist tradition, according to the story.

We drove to the east coast one weekend to visit some friends in Kuantan, a scenic town with a postcard-beautiful beach where the palm trees grew right next to the water in pearly white sand. We sorely needed to get away from the pressure of constant activities, just the five of us, but made the mistake of letting our plans be known. Ah Tec and Ah Tai invited themselves to go with us to see relatives there. We couldn't say no, of course, so the five of them piled in with us, bringing live chickens to help out with the meals. Ah Tec brought back a good supply of Kuantan's famous and smelly dried salt fish. We enjoyed the trip anyway, and they deserved the treat, which didn't cost us a thing.

We took another trip, an excursion up the river on a long boat to a national preserve near the Thai border. We left two-year-old Daniel with Esa and took Mark and Paul. Occasionally, we came to a shallow place in the river where Thomas and I had to get out and wade while the guides lifted boat, boys, and all and portaged across the rapids. The rocks were so slippery in places that Thomas and I had to cross on all fours. We got the giggles while the guides stared at us, mouths agape.

We had made a late start that morning, and it took all afternoon to reach the scenic cabin on the riverbank where we spent the night. Though it was a bit late for it, the guides took us along a hewn path into the jungle to a blind where we might see some wild animals. We didn't see a thing; and by the time we started back, it was dusk. I noticed that the guides held their machetes tightly and looked from side to side as if prepared for any emergency. We arrived safely and prepared supper in the wood stove in which the guides had made a fire, but not before we picked the leeches off our legs and feet. It was pleasant to go to sleep to the cheerful gurgling of the river. We returned safely home the next day after being in the wilderness for 30 hours, having seen no other humans besides our guides.

We took a trip the next year to the east coast to watch the giant sea turtles make their annual visit ashore to lay their eggs. Our dear friend Betty Snead and her two youngest children accompanied us. Going on a Thursday night was a mistake because it was the day before the Muslim Sabbath. While the government and businesses in the rest of the country observed the weekend with the Western world, on the extremely conservative eastern coast, things closed up on Friday. There were hordes of people headed in the same direction as we to watch the turtles come in.

Dozens of small islands dotting the coastline presented another complication: We had to take a ferry from one island to the next, waiting in line for an hour or more for our turn.

The time was not wasted though, for Betty kept us enthralled by telling us her life story. She and her husband and children were missionaries in Laos when the Japanese invaded. They escaped with some other missionaries deep into the jungle where they lived for several months before being discovered and taken to a concentration camp in the Philippines. There, they suffered much misery and hardship, including malnutrition. Their captors issued unpolished rice, which the prisoners had to clean and husk before cooking. Had they cooked it with the husk on, it would have torn up their insides.

Betty told of the day the Allies arrived. They heard rumors of the coming of the Allies and so had the Japanese, who trained the machine guns on the prisoners with the intention of mowing them all down just as the rescuers arrived. The Allies arrived earlier than expected, however, and freed the captives who returned home on an American battleship where they began to recuperate. On the ship, they were fed two soft-boiled eggs for the first few meals in order for their systems to adjust to normal food. "I wanted a dozen of those soft-boiled eggs!" Betty told us.

They returned as missionaries to Malaya after the end of the war and a period of rest and recuperation. The husband died in a plane crash on the way to bring the two oldest daughters from their school in India for Christmas. Betty went home for a while and had recently returned, at the request of the Mission Board, to be the housemother for the children's hostel in Singapore. What a story.

We arrived at the beach, finally, and found the place swarming with people. We spread our mats on the snow-white sand and lay down to rest, awaiting sleep. The moon was encircled by a rainbow, and the sky was bedecked with stars. A cloud occasionally drifted over the moon, and the sea was as calm as glass. We awoke at about 4:00 in the morning to shouts from the crowd, for here came the ladies to deposit their young. Six feet and over, scaly and clumsy, they grunted and pawed as they laid their eggs in the sand. We imagined, if they had been human, how indignant they would have felt over our intrusion into their privacy and were dismayed to see people jumping on the poor creatures and otherwise tormenting them.

During our second year in Raub, the theological college in Singapore assigned a young woman to us whom they had trained to teach kindergarten. She started a class in a classroom at the girls' school just a few steps from our house. Paul, who was five years old by then, couldn't wait to start. He was up early on that first day, dressed in his little white shirt, red shorts, and a red bow tie, and was at school before the teacher arrived. At the 10 o'clock recess time, however, he came home. He changed clothes and announced that he was finished with school—he had more important things to do.

I knew it would be impossible to keep him in the class because of the many distractions so did not insist. He had too much fun around the house, climbing on a jungle gym in the yard and teasing the gardener who was Tamil and didn't speak English. The gardener taught Paul a few words, including *jahat*, which means "naughty" in Tamil. Paul would squat under a window near where the gardener was working outside and jump up, shouting "jahat!" then duck back down. The gardener, in turn, would shout back, "jahat!" Oh, they had great fun, and it was probably a more valuable experience for Paul than being shut up in a classroom all morning.

The town had a mosque where the Muezzin chanted the call to prayer five times a day over a sound system that we could hear from as far away as our house.

We played on the school *padang* (playing field) below our house often, and that's where I taught Mark to ride his bicycle and where the boys played ball. There was a large, handsome man who passed by almost daily, driving a colorful bullock cart with a gracefully curved roof. He headed toward town in the morning and came back in the late afternoon with the cart loaded with hay. I knew he was Punjabi, for he wore the traditional turban and had a great, graying beard. His bullocks were two huge water buffalo. We always waved; but one day, he stopped and dismounted the cart, wanting to know who I was and what I was doing there. We tried to communicate even though we had no common language. No, that's wrong; a frequent nod and a smile said enough.

The monsoon rains came in June, July, and August, beginning with a steady drizzle and waning toward the end. It poured day and night without letup in mid-season and made it hard to dry the laundry and created a lot of mold and colder temperatures. We varnished our books and kept our camera and film in an airtight container with silica gel to keep them dry.

It usually rained about 4:30 in the afternoon when it wasn't monsoon season, and I looked forward to this time each day. I made a cup of tea and sat on the top step beneath the carport and watched from our hill as the rain came down. It cleared up after 20 minutes or so, as quickly as it had started, and the sun came out, creating a shimmering world around me. When the monsoon rains had not swelled the river too much, we went swimming in the river where I taught Mark and Paul to swim.

We could purchase most of what we needed right there in Raub except for pharmaceuticals. The nearest drug store was 80 steep, winding miles to Kuala Lumpur. When we went there, we saw American friends and went to a place called Cold Storage, where we could get a real hamburger, fresh milk, and our kind of ice cream.

I had a toothache once that was treated locally, with poor results. After a week of suffering, we drove to Kuala Lumpur where a wisdom tooth was pulled. What a relief!

On our trips to Kuala Lumpur, we stopped often in a town called Ben Tong where Ted Simmons, a bachelor missionary, ran a boys' boarding school. Ted thought it was a great joke to instruct the cook to put extra peppers into the food, making it so hot that even the locals couldn't eat it. We tried not letting him know we were coming until just before leaving our house. Alas, he would still have time to "hotten up" the food. Surprising him by not calling ahead didn't work either, and finally we learned to arrive after the meal was on the table.

I spent much time in the office next to our kitchen, helping Thomas with his paperwork, which he didn't seem able to handle without my assistance. I realized many years later that the more I took on, the more dependent he became. I realized too late that by doing his bidding and by placating him, I had trained him to make unreasonable demands upon me. In turn, he had trained me to comply with his demands in order to keep the peace.

"Look, I am not a machine," I said often. "I am a human being. Sometimes I'm tired, sometimes I'm sick, and sometimes I just don't happen to want to do what you are demanding." At the same time, I continued doing his bidding. I did not realize that I had a right to say "no."

Ever vigilant for some slight, Thomas became angry and disillusioned with the budget committee when they turned down his request for an adding machine. He had taken a course in seminary in conducting community surveys, and he desperately wanted to conduct one in our community, for which he would need the device to do the statistics.

After this, Thomas said that if he had the money, he would have us return to the States right away. He wasn't happy in this little insignificant corner of the world anyway, where life was slow and simple. He longed to be in Singapore where there was much action of he could be a part, and, after some negotiations, we were transferred. I said goodbye and packed, and we moved. It was to be a disaster for us.

Life is a smorgasbord if you dare to partake.

CHAPTER EIGHT

SINGAPORE

Here we were in the fascinating, sophisticated city of Singapore. We had thought we would be assigned to teach at Trinity Theological College; but it was decided at the last minute that we should pastor a young church in Sarangoon Gardens, a fairly new subdivision. Thomas could still be involved in the greater issues.

The residential area was large, with small duplexes that had been hastily and cheaply built with small rooms that had no closets or shelves, even in the kitchen. About half of the population in the area were British and Australian military and the other half, indigenous people.

Some of our neighbors were a rather rough crowd with a lot of small children. I purchased a small, plastic wading pool for my boys and had a hard time keeping other children out of it. One day I had to intervene when I looked out and saw my neighbor lifting her daughter over the fence without asking.

Our church constituency was mostly bright young Chinese with some Tamil people and Australian military personnel. Many were professionals with much leadership ability of their own. We were impressed by the fact that they had built the church, patterned after the U. S. Air Force Academy chapel, with their own money rather than depending on the mission to do it. This gave them an attitude of independence and, sometimes, a degree of belligerence toward missions.

Mark and Paul entered the American School, a highly rated program that had a policy requiring that 50% of the students be indigenous in order to maintain diversity. Paul was resistant the first day and ran after me when I started to leave.

"Paul, children all over the world attend school, and it is the law here, just like in the States," I explained. No matter, he wanted me to stay, which I did for an hour or two every day for a while until he was adjusted.

He sailed through his subjects while Mark struggled with math. I believe it was because Mark didn't quite complete second grade, our having left Raub in September before he would have finished the school year in December. He had also changed from one school system to another drastically different one, but he eventually caught up and did well. I later taught a "religious knowledge" class once a week for third- and fourth-graders, for which I put together my own materials rather than use old, outdated ones.

I drove the boys to and from school on most days and thoroughly enjoyed it. They asked questions that made for many, meaningful discussions on those trips. Cell phones, iPods, handheld computer games, etc., were not a distraction.

As I was driving across the city one day to pick up the boys, I approached an intersection where I was headed down a steep hill, intending to turn left. On my right, I saw a Chinese man pedaling a pedicab, uphill. This was a vehicle built like a bike with a buggy-type seat on the back that could carry two adult passengers or three small ones. I had the right-of-way but could see that he was struggling to get up the hill and that if he to wait for me, he would have to start from a dead stop with his fare of three children. I noticed his huge calf muscles and veins bulging from the strain and stopped and waited. As he passed, he gave me the universal thumbs-up sign with a big smile and nod of thanks. We spoke different languages, but some languages are global; that day we connected just fine.

There was flooding once during the December, January, and February monsoons when the tide was high, making it impossible to get through to the school in the car. Thomas and a friend left the cars parked some distance away and waded in to fetch the children. They brought them out, one by one, on their shoulders, and all got home safely.

Celebration!

Until Kennedy's assassination, we had not realized in what high esteem he was held. People of all walks of life there mourned him deeply; I thought they could not have been more grieved if one of their own popular leaders had died so tragically. At a memorial service, I heard a woman say, "We have all lost him."

Nor did I realize how strongly Americans felt about him and his family. It seemed that as the days went by, the more I read in the papers about the tragedy, the sadder I felt. Being a wife about the same age as Jackie and a mother with small children, I wept for her. She proved herself a great lady during this time, in my opinion.

Mark became seriously interested in the presidents after Kennedy's death, so I purchased a children's encyclopedia, which he studied for hours at a time. If you wanted to know who the 24th president was or how many had died in office, you could just ask him. His favorite president was Abraham Lincoln, with George Washington a close second.

I enrolled Mark and Paul into a judo class that met twice a week, buying the special uniforms that were required, and drove them to and from class.

Paul was interested in building things and whenever he saw some sticks, junk, or pieces of lumber, he would say, "Why, I could build (whatever he had thought of) out of that!" We bought him a little set of tools to encourage him.

Our darling Daniel was finally toilet trained by his third birthday but slow in everything. He was having trouble getting along with his brothers because he did not know how to play with them. He was also driving me nuts pouring things out—sun lotion, detergent—down the sink they would go, slowly, as he watched in fascination. He loved gathering things into a bag, including papers and pencils off my desk, bottles and bottle caps, spools of thread and parts off my sewing machine.

There were no child psychologists in the city at the time, so I took Daniel to a pediatrician for evaluation. He did some informal things such as showing him pictures from a magazine and asking him questions about them. The doctor concluded that while Dan would never be first in his class, his intelligence was probably normal. He also added that perhaps Dan was just a bit lazy and that kindergarten may be of help even though he was still quite young. I knew better than to think Dan was lazy but did put him into kindergarten, which was good for him.

I read a lot to my children when they were young. We piled into the bed at night with a dozen books; and when I announced that it was time to go to sleep, they begged me to read some more—probably a ruse to stay up a little later—and it worked. When we finally were ready for sleep, we sang taps together—"Day is done; gone the sun, from the lake, from the hills, from the sky. All is well; safely rest; God is nigh." Instead of "God is nigh," Daniel would sing, "God is nice."

Thomas and two women from the Episcopal Diocese initiated Singapore's first interdenominational Christian worship service that included Catholics, Methodists, and Episcopalians. They rented a movie theater and had an overflow crowd of about 800 people with some standing in the back. Thomas was asked to make up the order of service and to lead the worship.

Hymns, litanies, the Lord's Prayer, the Nicene Creed, and a sermon were included; and no one expressed the view that any one group was compromising. It just felt good to be working together. One of the things that irked us about certain missionaries was the interdenominational competition, not so much from the more liberal denominations as from fundamentalist groups. They came behind us to tell local people that everyone except their own sect was going to hell! Especially the Methodist bishop.

Thomas headed up the Singapore Christian Social Services and lectured the Planned Parenthood Association on the subject of "What do the Major Religions in Singapore Believe about Family Planning?" This was long before abortion was an issue, of course. I spoke to the British servicemen's wives' club about my experiences in Malaya and was well received. We had noticed that many expatriates did not mingle with the local people very much but stayed within their own community, to their great loss.

Articles and pictures of the king and queen of Thailand were frequently in the news, especially when they visited Singapore. They were a gorgeous couple! The queen was described as one of the most beautiful queens in the world and one of the 10 best dressed. Her title was "Her Serene Highness, Queen Sirikit," which inspired me to want to be serene like her. I still have her picture in my belongings.

On the noisy streets of Singapore, we saw conveyances of every variety—bicycles loaded with everything imaginable— stacks of cartons of eggs, lumber, crates of fruits and vegetables, mattresses, caged birds, balloons, baskets, straw for the animals, pots and pans, and one or more passengers. Some were piled so high that one couldn't see the cyclist. There were trucks, pull carts—some covered and some not—oxcarts, wagons, motor scooters, and taxis of all makes and vintages in the streets and every kind of boat in the harbor.

Some of the finer stores were enclosed and air-conditioned while other shops opened onto the sidewalk, with goods hanging from the doors and outside on the buildings' façades. They displayed clothes, fabrics, electronics, toys, umbrellas, hats, souvenirs, books, tape recordings, fruit, vegetables, chickens with their heads still on, sausages, pork, and beef. One could get a haircut and have shoes repaired on the sidewalk and buy anything in the world duty-free.

One street belonged exclusively to food venders in the evening. They came with their push carts at dusk when the place lit up and came to life. We went there frequently with friends to eat delicious food of all kinds and to watch the sights. Costumes from every country and culture could be seen—Western dresses and business suits, native costumes and workday outfits—and many languages heard.

People who lived in upstairs quarters hung their wash on poles to dry, hanging them out of the windows like flagpoles.

Visitors to Singapore could observe artisans painting, weaving, carving, sewing, arranging flowers, or making pottery and could attend concerts or visit the zoo and historical sites. They could visit and worship in churches, synagogues, temples, and mosques. We just didn't have time to do it all.

Singapore has grown and changed drastically since our time there. It has become ultra-modern, more industrialized, and more cosmopolitan. I yearn to go back.

Two week-long periods of riots interrupted the peace, probably were more political than racial and probably were instigated by the Indonesians. They crippled the entire city. We were put under curfew and not allowed outside our house, even in the yard.

Imagine a huge city that never sleeps, teeming with people; now imagine that it is silent for the first time in its life. There was not a soul in sight, not a car in the streets. Think of all the vendors, cab drivers, and merchants who were idled.

Then, suddenly, the city's alive. Every 12 hours, for one hour, the curfew was lifted, and the whole city poured into the streets to take care of business.

People drove on the sidewalks, on the wrong side of the street; and in the market, they grabbed desperately at products to put into their baskets. It was interesting to observe human behavior, including my own, in an emergency. I grabbed a large squash that I would never have chosen, anything to fill my basket before the time was up.

Some friends drove quickly to our house during the break one day and stayed the 12 hours until they could return home. We had a real house party. There were bombings at the bank building where my dentist had his office, and two of the bank tellers were killed. We understood that this was all instigated by the communist element.

Thomas kept speaking up to say that the church should be heard on issues like this that affect society and was asked to write an article about it for the conference magazine, for which he was the associate editor. He suggested that Christians plan certain actions they would take to promote peace among the different communities and nationalities in Singapore. Some of the younger, sharper Malaysians saw the church as stagnant, uninvolved, and ineffectual and were trying to change that. Thomas saw that also and exercised great leadership in these areas. Some said later that he was five years too early, as some of his suggestions were taken more seriously after we left.

Singapore received its independence from England shortly after we arrived and joined with the Federation of Malaya, formerly a British colony, Sarawak (part of the Borneo island), and Sabah, in North Borneo, to form the Federation of Malaysia. This had been a long time coming, with many discussions, delays, and postponements. The communists opposed the merger because they feared that such unification would weaken them in Singapore, as it did.

There had long been much fear between the Chinese, who were more aggressive, and the Malays, who were more placid. Much jealousy resulted from Kuala Lumpur's practice of what we in the U. S. call "affirmative action." Chinese students graduating from the university with higher grades were passed over for jobs and government positions that were made available to Malays with less impressive academic achievements. But by the time of *merdeca* (independence), the merger was a reality. There was much celebration over several days, with much work yet to be done.

Now the issues that the Church had to address were freedom of religion for all people, including the Malays and aboriginals—whether or not Malaysians were ready to take responsibility for a more autonomous church, whether or not the church was ready for more autonomous Malaysians—questions about labor unions, greater justice for criminals, and the church's role in the newly developing, industrialized Singapore. But one main bone of contention between the governments still was the special privileges given to Malays because they were more "native" to the land. The Singapore general elections came next and returned Lee Kuan Yew's government, opposed by the communists, to the position he has held since first being elected in 1959. I understand that the government has become stricter than when we were there.

We carried on the usual church programs and Thomas branched out. He visited Parliament in Singapore and took a night train to Kuala Lumpur to observe Parliament there and to get a taste of what was happening on the mainland. He also lectured at the theological college on "A Pastor's Role in Community Life" and "The Local Church Organized for Social Action."

A carload of kids from our youth group in Raub came and stayed a few days after we had been in Singapore a few months. They thoughtfully provided their own groceries for the most part, which they cooked at our house, paid for any long-distance phone calls, and helped clean up. They enjoyed the boys, and of course, we loved having them. We learned from them that Ah Tai, our next-door-neighbor in Raub, had encountered a large python in her chicken house and killed it by beating it with a bamboo cane. She butchered the serpent, according to the story, sold the meat, and kept the skin as a souvenir. I was always amazed at her ingenuity and was even more so after this.

We were impressed with this congregation; they had such energy and vision. It didn't take long for us to become involved with the usual church activities, feeling very close to a number of members and their families.

Then, after only four months, the bomb dropped. Some of the strongest members of the church had taken an intense dislike for Thomas and in one particular meeting ganged up against him, listing all his shortcomings and their grievances against him. He was pale and trembling when he returned home that night; and the first thing he said was, "Do I look as if I have been pulverized?" I tried to comfort him, but he pulled away.

Celebration!

We both tried to facilitate some kind of reconciliation, to no avail. I talked personally with some of the church members, defending my husband, and hoping they would have a change of heart. They had certainly been unfair and cruel in the way they treated their pastor. Even so, they said later that we could have worked things out if Thomas had not been so belligerent and intransigent. I was to ask him a few years later in a similar situation, "Do you want to reach an understanding with these people, or do you simply want to fight?"

I was expecting our fourth child, and this was especially difficult for me. For a little relief and relaxation, Thomas and I began having dinner at a nice restaurant before attending lectures on Wednesday nights at the University. We heard several speakers on local and worldwide issues, and Thomas audited some other courses. And we took a two-week trip to Borneo, which I will tell about in the next chapter.

Justus was born on June 25, 1964, after our trip to Borneo, at Glen Eagles Hospital with a Western-trained staff—a very nice place to have a baby. It was the first time I gave birth without medication for pain; it was not easy, but worth it because of my greater clarity and his greater well-being. While I was in hard labor, I heard the nurse talking to the doctor, who was at his office. "I think it'll be about 20 more minutes, so you may want to come on over," she advised.

"No! Tell him to come right now," I called to her. "We're not doing this for 20 more minutes!" We did, of course, and soon, out he popped. "It's a boy!" the nurse exclaimed.

Although I had been in pain for about five hours, it was no time after the delivery until I had forgotten all that. I held the precious bundle in my arms and exclaimed, "Oh, what a wonderful experience! I wish I could have another." This illustrates how time heals pain.

I enjoyed my stay in the hospital and rather dreaded going home. Our hospitalization was extended because of our babies' history of blood incompatibility and antibodies. Justus was fine.

That week, I caught up on my correspondence, prepared birth announcements, and went to a daily exercise class.

The nurse came at about 5:30 each morning and brought a pot of tea, English-style, with cream and sugar. She opened the windows and drapes to let in wonderfully cool morning air, and I sipped tea as dawn tiptoed in. When I was almost finished, here she came with my fabulous baby for me to nurse, a memory I still relish today. After the nurse took him away, I got up, took a shower, put on makeup, and got back to bed in time for breakfast. Can one blame me for not wanting to go home?

Thomas brought the other boys every evening to visit us. They adored Justus from Day One; and after I was back at home, Mark was good help.

We hired Mary, age 27, as an amah, before Justus was born; and she and her family were with us until time for our return to the States. She and her husband were Buddhists, originally from Burma, now Myanmar, where they attended Catholic schools and learned to speak English. All nine of their children were beautiful and healthy, with pearly white teeth, even though they were poor and ate little meat. Mary had had her tubes tied after the last child, for which I commended her. She and I became good friends. The husband, unemployed, stayed home and took care of the children. And drank.

We asked the bishop to transfer us after about four more miserable months in Sarangoon Gardens and were assigned to Barker Road Methodist Church, closer to town. The parsonage and the Methodist Anglo-Chinese Boys' School were next to the church. This was another young congregation of active, sharp people, Chinese and Indian mostly, many of whom were graduates of the boys' school.

Some other missionaries occupied the parsonage at the time, so we lived around the corner temporarily in a large colonial-style house that the mission had once used as the children's hostel. We occupied only the first floor and I began to figure out how to keep the huge living room from seeming like a tomb.

Celebration!

I arranged the furniture into conversational groups, creating a nice effect.

We had so much extra room upstairs that we were able to take in two women missionaries and their children who were refugees from Indonesia, where there was trouble with the communists. Their husbands stayed behind but were unharmed, and in time, things there settled down.

Wanting to be closer to the action, we moved into the parsonage as soon as the other occupants moved out. A traditional house, it was charming, with the corners of the roof curved upward Chinese-style. This discouraged evil spirits, who travel in straight lines only. The whole living room opened up onto a patio and yard where we had orchids, ferns, hibiscus, and other luscious flowers.

We lived on a high hill, looking down at the school's playing field. Beyond that was Barker Road, the main thoroughfare linking the island to the mainland. It was down this road that the Japanese had come when they took over Singapore. The British had thought they would invade by way of the sea so were unprepared for an invasion by land.

Residents told us many stories about that day, from the time they saw the tanks coming across the causeway, down Barker Road, and into the city. They recalled their feelings of dread and doom as they watched. They told first-hand stories of unimaginable atrocities during the occupation. Our friend, Kim, who was partially crippled, told us this story:

"I entered a movie theatre one afternoon in my hometown and sat down in an empty seat. A Japanese soldier, who had left the same seat to go to the bathroom, returned and found me sitting there. He picked me up and threw me out into the street, breaking my hip, and went back into the theater. Because of lack of medical services, the hip didn't heal properly. That's why I'm crippled today."

"China Town" was deep inside the City of Singapore. We thought this was interesting, as Singapore is a mostly-Chinese city. The oldest people, the oldest buildings, the oldest architecture, and oldest commerce were to be found in that original section of the city. We engaged a guide to take us and another couple one evening on a walking tour into the area.

First, we entered a dark, spooky place, a square bounded by old buildings with ancient designs. Food venders, with their pushcarts, sold chicken, pork, rice, dumplings, stir-fried vegetables, curry, and soup. Blue-gray smoke from the charcoal grills stung our noses and made our eyes water. A frame over the soup cart displayed pictures that illustrated what kinds of soups were available—chicken, fish, pork, beef, rat, eel, snake, and dog. I wrote my parents, "We passed on before we passed out!"

There was a group of old men with thin, gray hair and long, scraggly beards, squatting sleepily on their haunches on benches arranged in a little group. They paid a reader ten Malay cents per hour to read stories to them as they smoked opium, An American dime was worth three Malay ten-cent pieces. The government of Singapore prohibited the possession and use of opium except for those who were already addicted, and in that case, it was permitted.

Late that evening, we came to a large building that looked on the outside like a warehouse where there were rows of compartments—cubby holes—on the inside that reached all the way to the ceiling. Each space contained only a thin mattress and was just large enough for a human to crawl into and lie down. Poor and homeless people rented these sleeping quarters for eight hours at a time; and when the renter left after his time was up, another one took his place. Not to worry about pillows, blankets, or clean linen.

I read that much of the old city has been torn down by the government in its efforts to modernize, but that as a result of strong protest, they desisted and saved some of it.

Another treat we looked forward to was going to the harbor in the evening to eat satay, which we bought for ten cents apiece. This treat was made of thin slices of pork or chicken marinated in coconut milk, brown sugar, and spices. The slices were threaded onto thin bamboo skewers, six or eight inches long, and grilled over charcoal. The grilled meat was then dipped into a sauce made of peanuts, spices, chili peppers, ginger root, candied ginger, and soy sauce. Yummy!

We sat on the pier and watched as our chef squatted over his hibachi and prepared our meal, enjoyed the cool breeze coming across the water at twilight, and watched the boats come and go. The boys had an ongoing contest to see which one of them could eat the most servings. I believe Mark was the champion, at 40 sticks.

We brought Mary and her family with us on each of these moves as these older homes had servants' quarters. Her husband did not need to do all the cooking and child care with Mary close by, so we gave him the job of keeping the extensive yard.

He often beat Mary when he was drunk and didn't get any yard work done during those times. I had a big row with him one day about beating Mary, but he let me know that it was none of my business, that he had a right to beat his wife.

We joined the American Club nearby in order to have a place to swim. We were hesitant at first because of not wanting to seem "exclusive," but learned of the policy that called for a membership consisting of an equal number of Americans and Asians. We had tried the public pool, which was clean and adequate; but the Asian children, out of friendly curiosity, wouldn't leave our boys alone so that they didn't have any fun. They especially wanted to touch Paul's blond hair. We seldom ate at the club, because of the expense, but met and visited with interesting people around the pool, and it was a good place to cool off.

We had a fine year at Barker Road, with a vital young adult program that offered strong leadership and many active and dedicated teenagers. As the chaplain at the Methodist Anglo-Chinese Boys' School, Thomas conducted Religious Emphasis Week and provided counseling to any students who requested it. After the Religious Emphasis Week, we had Holy Week services.

We worked with another intern from the theological college while serving the Barker Road church.

The prime minister of Singapore, Lee Kuan Yew, is a graduate of this Methodist school. I once sat at the same table with him at an alumni dinner; but as I recall, he didn't pay much attention to me.

We presented a play on Good Friday that I directed, and I served a brunch on our patio for everyone on Easter Sunday. I had plenty of help, though, because many guests brought food and helped with the serving. As chairman of the Christian Education committee, I worked to help organize the educational program and train the teachers and wrote some material that was published for use in the Conference. We had an average of 100 worshippers on Sundays, and many more attended the other activities. These people were a delight to work with.

I cried the whole two weeks before we left to return home.

Now it was 1965, and our first term was to end soon.

We had to decide what to do for our year off. We could study, work, or do deputation work, which would have meant traveling all over the United States to tell of our work and to promote missions. The Mission Board would support us all the way, paying salary, travel expenses, and 100 percent medical coverage.

Thomas began putting out feelers for some opportunities in the areas of peace or civil rights because deputation work was not appealing. He inquired about a job with a peace organization in Chicago, from whom he received a reply to the effect that they hadn't the funds to hire him.

I asked him about a letter I had come across that he had written to them, offering to work without pay. His reply was alarming: "Well, maybe we can find someone who'll give us a place to live, and we wouldn't need much of anything else." Thomas also began talking about getting into a Ph.D. program.

What about the family's daily needs? What did our future hold?

I was busy planning the itinerary for our trip home, working with a travel agent. With a re-outfitting allowance and money we had saved, we intended to take three weeks along the way, and planning the details took a lot of time. At the same time, I prepared and organized the household for getting packed. I said to Thomas finally, "I need an address to put on these boxes and barrels."

Then one day, we received an overseas radio phone call from Dr. John King of Huston-Tillotson College in Austin, Texas, a predominantly Black school. He offered Thomas a teaching position. Dr. King knew Thomas's father personally and would hire him on that basis. Thomas accepted the offer after I agreed to it.

We both thought that the most important events were happening back home and we wanted to be a part of it. We also believed that it was time for the Civil Rights Movement to get off the streets and into the classroom, and that's where we believed we could make a difference.

The only problem for me was that our before-taxes salary would be $5,000. I had no idea how far that would go in 1965 for a family of six. But then we learned we could continue to get support from the Mission Board for a year, and the salary the college paid us by the college would go back to the Mission Board. That sounded more secure to me.

The Mission Board offered us another term, to be served in Sibu in Sarawak, part of the island of Borneo. It would be interesting and challenging to work among the Iban people, yet we both agreed that perhaps the most vital work was at home.

We would have a year to decide whether or not to remain with the Mission Board.

Our church community gave us an impressive send-off with a big party at the church, and a big crowd was at the airport to see us off. I cried all the way to Thailand.

In your heart and in your mind, bless everyone you meet.

CHAPTER NINE

BORNEO

Medical missionary friends who lived and worked in Sarawak, part of the island of Borneo, visited us when we lived in Raub and insisted we visit them in return. In April of 1964, with a baby due in June, we decided that if we were to go at all, it had to be soon. We couldn't take a baby to Borneo, and we would be returning home the next year. Was I taking a risk by going there with the baby due so soon? I had never had any trouble with early deliveries and knew that if that should happen, help would not be far away.

We flew from Singapore to Kuching, the capital, a two-and-a-half hour flight compared to a boat trip that would have taken four days. In Kuching, we stayed with missionary friends. We visited a museum that gave the history of Sarawak and the Ibans, the local tribe whom we were to visit, and saw some old shrunken heads and models of longhouses. Kuching was a lovely town, clean, with large buildings, and much bigger and more developed than we had expected.

We flew the next day from Kuching to Sibu and were met by one of Thomas's dad's old seminary classmates, Doug Coole, and his wife Mamie. They were gracious hosts. Doug had grown up in China as the son of missionaries and spoke the Fuchow dialect like a Fuchow Chinese. We enjoyed watching him stroll down the street like one of the locals, chatting with everyone he met. Fuchow is a very difficult dialect, we learned, and unless one grew up speaking that dialect, it was almost impossible to learn. Doug and Mamie had been missionaries in China, India, and Malaya and now had been in Sarawak for about 16 years. They were cordial and fascinating.

Celebration!

We stayed with the Cooles for two days before boarding a boat that would take us 90 miles upriver overnight to our destination, the town of Kapit, where our friends lived and worked at Christ Hospital. Beyond Sibu, the only travel was done on the river, unless the British helicopters had been called in. The Cooles packed thermos bottles of coffee, bottles of water, and food for us to have on the way, and we rented cabins with bunk beds for the 12-hour trip. The beds were covered with thin mattresses and were very uncomfortable for me especially, but I finally went to sleep that night to the sound of the slapping of water against the side of the boat and the chugging of the motor.

We awoke the next morning to the acrid smell of charcoal and breakfast being prepared on deck and soon spotted our enthusiastic friends waiting for us at the dock. The town consisted almost completely of the hospital with a small business district and some schools. Most of the nurses and one of the doctors were missionaries from the Philippines, and our doctor friend was American with a Filipino wife. Kapit was quiet and peaceful, quite a relief from the hustle of Singapore. With no roads, we walked everywhere, which was good for me in my condition. There were two vehicles in town, one of which was a Land Rover owned by the hospital.

The British military had moved in because of trouble from the communists in the Indonesian part of the island, bringing powerful vehicles for moving heavy equipment. Most of the soldiers were the famous Gurkhas from Nepal, professional fighters who, under a special agreement between the governments of England and Nepal, went anywhere the British government sent them. The local people appreciated the soldiers because they saw them as kind and helpful and because they protected them from the insurgents.

Twice during our visit, the military brought in sick people by helicopter. Otherwise, they would have had to come by boat, a trip taking several days, and most likely would not have come at all. While we were there, a little girl died of amoebic dysentery she had had for two weeks before they flew her in. But it was too late. The American doctor, Norvin Shuman, worked over her for two days but couldn't save her. It was very sad, for the parents were an older couple whose five children had all died of the same sickness. Norvin told us that between the time of conception and the first birthday, 50 percent of the children died. Let us hope that much progress has been made since then.

One of the main reasons for infant mortality was a certain practice surrounding childbirth. It was customary for the maternal grandmother of the baby to push on the abdomen of the mother in order to get the baby out. In this agonizing process, they often ended up killing both the mother and the child. As word spread that the baby could be delivered at Christ Hospital without such suffering, others came for delivery when possible.

The hospital staff told us that when the grandmother accompanied the expectant mother, they could tell just how much she wanted to get her hands on her daughter in order to push the baby out. We were also told that because of the high infant mortality rate, the Ibans doted on their children excessively. In addition, because of the prevalence of sexually transmitted diseases, many have difficulty in conceiving.

This leads me to describe their courtship and marriage customs. We were told that the unmarried women slept on the veranda where the unmarried men could come to "visit." When a couple, by mutual agreement, decided to marry, it was worked out with the council. If a girl became pregnant, she could inform the man, who could marry her if he chose to, but had the right to decline. The girl would be hurt, of course, if he didn't want her, but there was no stigma over the pregnancy. There were plenty of people in the longhouse to care for all the children. If the man declined to marry her, he lost his "visiting" rights; and if, after that, he so much as stepped onto her mat, she could call out his name, and he would be required to marry her.

Celebration!

The longhouses with verandas across their entire front reminded me of very primitive motels on stilts. The structure was built at the edge of the river and on stilts because of periodic flooding, caused by the river god. There were no stairs as we know them, not even a ladder or railing to hold on to. A very large log with notches cut out for steps was simply leaned up against the veranda. We have a snapshot of me, seven months pregnant, climbing one of those logs on all fours.

Each family had one door opening onto the porch with a section of several rooms behind each door. The population was calculated by the number of doors; if each "door" housed 10 people and there were 10 doors, one could assume that there were 100 people in the longhouse.

Each longhouse had a headman chosen by the people, and he had to be a very good man, they told us. He settled disputes with the help of a council, a system that appeared to work very well. The man who governed all of a group of longhouses within a certain area was called a *penghulu*. This position was not hereditary but elected. There was a man who was head of all the *penghulus*. The *penghulu* of the Ibans that we visited was a Christian whose name was Tangmangong Juga. We attended the wedding of his son and took pictures of them. Besides Ibans, Malays, and Chinese, there were several other tribes of people—Kayans, Kenyahs, and Kelabits.

We went from Kapit by longboat one hour up the river on Sunday morning to a longhouse for worship. We arrived there at about 10:00, which was time for the service to start, and the indigenous pastor was already there. We sat cross-legged and chatted while some smoked or read newspapers as we waited one hour for everyone to arrive. Not that they had far to come; the service was specifically for those in this longhouse. They were not concerned about being on time, obviously. The Iban pastors called each longhouse a "point" in their circuit and visited each longhouse to hold services. Sometimes, the entire longhouse decided, as a group, to become Christians, all at once.

Once the service finally got under way, it was very similar to our services back at home, except that it was in the Iban language and there were plenty of chickens, pigs, and dogs participating. The headman invited us into his room for tea after the service. I feared that I would fall through the floor at any moment, for it was made of bamboo with big cracks in between, and the whole house seemed precarious on those poles. In fact, we were told that this house was old and that the people were in the process of building a new one, although they didn't seem to be making much progress.

The furnishings in the rooms were scant, consisting of a few cooking utensils and baskets for fishing and carrying things. I thought that housekeeping must be easy, but not so. The women were the ones who did most of the farming while the men were hunting, fishing, or sitting around talking. During the harvest season, however, everyone went to the rice fields, and many of them slept and ate there until the entire crop was gathered. The longhouse was practically deserted during that time, and the people had no time for other things. We were told that the little girl who died had been neglected because it was harvest time and the parents could not get away to take her to the hospital.

The Ibans wore little clothing; the men sported only short pants and sometimes a strip of cloth around the waist and between the legs. Most of the women were bare-breasted, wearing only sarongs, but some of them put on tops or bras on our account. Many of the men and women had extensive tattoos that covered much of the body. Some of the designs had significant religious or spiritual meaning or were related to certain superstitions. We were glad the missionaries had not interfered with the local dress, only with the customs that were harmful. Many of the women had long, draping earlobes as a result of wearing heavy bangles in the ears since birth.

We loved the Ibans. They were so open, so simple, warmhearted and gracious. They loved and appreciated the missionaries and all they were doing, especially the fact that the missionaries had taught many of them to read and write.

During our visit to Kapit, we took another trip by longboat to visit an agricultural mission called Nanga Mujong, managed by Tom Harris and his wife, African-American missionaries. Their two adopted daughters, one Asian and one Eurasian, were in school in Singapore and living at the children's hostel.

The rides on the river in the longboats were lovely, if hard on my backside. Upriver Sarawak reminded me very much of Pahang where we lived after first arriving in Malaya. In some places that were less mountainous, I remarked that it could be some park in Florida.

Back in Sibu, Doug Coole took us in his speedboat to visit some other agricultural missions where agricultural missionaries taught the local farmers how to improve their rubber and rice crops. We also visited the Methodist Theological College in Sibu where they were training young pastors to take over leadership and where we attended chapel services. Then, it was goodbye to Sarawak.

To discover what your attachments are,
what you think you have to have,
the way you insist things have to be,
what makes you dissatisfied,
get out of your comfort zone.

CHAPTER TEN

RETURNING HOME

It was August of 1965 and time to return home. We took three weeks to make the trip, using our re-outfitting allowance and money we had saved. We spent a few days in Bangkok, where we stayed at a hostel for travelers. We went to the floating market, visited old temples where we purchased temple rubbings, and attended some entertaining programs that included dance and music.

We met an older woman at the hostel, who was taking a whirlwind trip around the world. She said she thought they had stopped in Singapore but couldn't quite remember. I conjectured that she and the other women in her group were widows going around the world on their dead husbands' insurance money. She asked me who we were and where we were going. I'm sure she wondered how a young couple with four children, including a one-year-old, could afford to travel like this.

After I explained that we had been doing a project for the Methodist Board of World Missions, she said, "Oh, how wonderful you are; you have sacrificed so much and suffered such hardships!"

"No, no. We haven't sacrificed at all," I said. "The only hardship was being so far away from our families, and we've actually gained much more than we gave."

"Oh, you say that because you are so dedicated!" she insisted, undaunted and wanting to put me into her preconceived "box" and keep me there. I gave up.

We visited New Delhi and were riding in a taxi when we saw an electronic sign on a newspaper building that read, "SINGAPORE SECEDES!" We weren't surprised, for there had too much fear between the two governments. Singapore then became a separate nation-state with its own ambassadors and representatives to the United Nations.

We visited the magnificent Taj Mahal in Agra, where we removed our shoes and left them at the door. The mausoleum was built in the 17th century to honor Muntaz Mahal, the beloved wife of the fifth emperor, Shah Jahan. We stayed long enough that evening to see its glorious opalescence in the moonlight. Agra was a poor, dirty, and gray-looking city as I recall. I was interested in the fact that there was a luxurious, air-conditioned Hilton Hotel there and that guests were transported to and from the shrine in air-conditioned buses. I wondered whether they were so well insulated from the culture that they missed something of the experience.

We went to Cairo after India, and stayed in a Class B hotel where the staff was not friendly and food not appetizing. Mark got sick and threw up in front of the wrought iron elevator. I did laundry in the bathroom sink and hung clothes in the open windows where birds liked to roost. We were using semi-disposable diapers that were not nearly as convenient as Pampers, which came along too late for my babies.

The stairway of the Great Pyramid was low, so we climbed all the way up, bent over as if bowing to the long-dead Pharaoh. I believe it was planned that way. The guide kept Justus in his taxi.

We rode camels and went by taxi through Bedouin territory on our way to the Dead Sea. We simply waved as we passed their tents. Our driver warned us that if we stopped, our hosts would expect us to have tea with them—not a good idea. We swam in the Dead Sea that was so thick it was like swimming in maple syrup. There was a little resort there where we had some refreshments and enjoyed conversations with the guide, who was well-spoken and modern in his outlook. When we asked about his family, he reported that they had two children and were not planning to have any more.

We went to Jerusalem next, first to the Jordan side, then the Israel side. The policy of the Arab nations at that time was that if one's passport showed that he had been to Israel previously, he was not allowed in, so we saved Israel until last. In Jerusalem, we did some shopping, visited the Garden of Gethsemane, walked along the Via Dolorosa where Jesus carried the cross, saw a place that could have been his tomb, and went to Bethlehem to see the shrine over what is supposedly his birthplace.

I wondered, *How can* anything be *so old?*

The children were marvelous travelers.

There was no extra charge for a side trip within a certain number of sky miles, so Thomas and the two older boys branched off for quick visits to Amsterdam and Moscow, an opportunity too good to pass up. I had foreseen that I would be ready to alight somewhere at this point and planned to go on with Daniel and Justus to New York.

My plane touched down in Rome, where they took on food that evidently disagreed with me, for a few hours later, I began to feel sick. I thought some hot tea might help and rang for the attendant. But this was August, and the plane was packed with American travelers returning home and dying for a drink. Such a large crowd gathered at the attendants' station that the pilot instructed everyone to return to their seats because they were throwing the plane out of balance.

The attendant answered my call after a couple of hours and graciously took Justus for a while so I could get some rest. Daniel, as always, was sweet and cooperative and traveled very well. In New York, my in-laws took me to a hotel, gave me some kind of sedative, and took the boys away. I awoke the next day, fully rested and recovered, happy to be back on my native ground.

Thomas and the boys arrived a couple of days later. In Moscow, where it had been quite chilly, their hotel did not provide enough blankets and they slept in all their clothes. The tickets they were given for food and other purchases ran out, and they had to pay extra for their meals. They, too, were happy to be back in America.

We spent a few days in New York for rest, physicals, and debriefing. Before leaving Singapore, we ordered a Volkswagen microbus from Germany just like the one we had in Malaya. It was delivered in the U. S. under a special arrangement for Americans overseas. We picked it up and had it cleaned and serviced.

Now we were on our way to Georgia to visit my parents and the old homestead after four years. I had no idea what kind of reception I was going to receive because Mama had written some hostile letters in response to my comments about Martin Luther King.

When we arrived at the farm, I discovered that some of her relatives in Savannah had taken issue over my remarks. Although she basically agreed with me on the issues of race, she was angry with me for speaking out and causing her relatives to criticize me. I felt hurt and confused. What did she expect of me? When I visited the family in Savannah, the reception was strange, to say the least, and it became more so when we informed them that we were on the way to Austin, Texas, to teach and work at a predominantly Black college.

Some of the people in my home church gave us a warm welcome, but the officials were wary and did not permit us to speak of our experiences overseas. Nor did any of our other supporting churches in the South.

I believe they were afraid of what we might say about civil rights and didn't want us stirring up trouble. They were right. We would have stirred up trouble!

When we take a stand, we have to be willing to pay the price.

CHAPTER ELEVEN

LIFE IN AUSTIN, 1965-1971

We left for Austin, Texas, after a stressful week at home and arrived in four days, on a Saturday. This was the middle of August, and the hot wind reminded me of India. Classes would begin in two weeks. We spent the first night at the home of Dr. and Mrs. John King and attended their all-Black church with them the next day.

We lived for two weeks in one of the dormitories until we could find a place to live. We had $500. Since this was the middle of August, we would not receive a paycheck until the end of September. We had to rent a house, buy school clothes for the older boys, buy a washing machine and a few pieces of furniture.

Sears allowed us to open an account based on Dr. King's word, so we bought enough things to get started. The precious house-mother of the dorm in which we were staying learned of our situation and whispered to me, "Come with me. I can give you some furniture."

I hired a truck, which she filled with some old furniture from the demolished home economics building. Among the things was a kitchen table just like the ones our grandmothers had in their kitchens. We had three chairs and took turns eating. Later, when I was able to purchase a real table and chair set, I cut the legs off that old table and made it into a coffee table by painting and antiquing it. I bought two bunk beds for the boys from a used furniture store, and Thomas and I slept on a new mattress on the floor for several months. We removed the middle seat from the microbus to use as a sofa in the living room and reminded visitors that they were sitting on an "imported sofa."

I refinished almost all of that junk eventually and used it for many years.

A few weeks after we arrived in Austin, unbeknownst to me, Thomas resigned us from the Mission Board. He was resentful toward the Mission Board and the church in general, and I suppose this was his way of getting back at them.

Now, we had no medical benefits, no funds for travel, and no financial backing. I felt adrift on the open sea with no paddle and no place of refuge. Reluctantly, I put my two young ones into daycare and began working in the college business office part-time.

We had just the one car, so I drove back to the college at the end of the day to pick Thomas up. I liked my job and my boss, Paul Bailey, who was quite easy to work with and appreciative of my work.

I enrolled as a sales representative for the *World Book Encyclopedia*, also, and made calls at night. My initial incentive was to earn enough credits to qualify for the complete educational program for the boys—the World Book Encyclopedia, dictionary, globe, the *Childcraft* set, and a "teaching machine." After I achieved that, I went on to make a little more money, selling mostly to friends and staff at the college and church. I became more familiar with East Austin, mostly populated by minorities, than with the rest of the city.

Thomas was assigned to teach five courses, mostly sociology, that first semester, none of which he had ever taught before. When he was not sleeping or in class, he "hibernated" to prepare for the next day's classes. He was an excellent teacher, much appreciated by the students and by Dr. King. I, too, enjoyed relating to the students as they came by the office to pay on their account or line up for meal tickets. We had some meaningful discussions when students came to our house for coffee and dessert. I believe they felt free to tell of their experiences of discrimination and their hopes for greater civil rights. I joined the students in a candlelight vigil on the grounds of the

Capitol when Martin Luther King, Jr. was assassinated. Thomas was out of town that day, as I recall.

As soon as we were settled, I began looking for a place where we could have Daniel evaluated. I found the Child Guidance Center in the phone book and made an appointment. It took several months of interviews and assessments before we had any final diagnosis or plan of action. I kept calling the agency to determine the next step because they were slow in getting back to me. By the next summer, it was determined that he had some organic brain damage and would qualify for special education. I felt overwhelmed.

We had to decide now what school to put Daniel into. We knew of an excellent school in a fine neighborhood with a good special education program that sounded ideal. It meant that Daniel would not have to ride in a special little bus to a different school from the other boys. The problem was the high cost of real estate in that area.

Then, through a cousin, we found the perfect little three-bedroom house on Cherry Lane that we could afford, with a little help from my dad, and it was not far from the school.

Daniel did quite well with dear Mrs. Dornberger, his special education teacher for three years. His classmates admired him because he was good-looking, well-coordinated, and athletic. He was also quiet and passive in contrast to others who were hyperactive. I left work at 2:00 in the afternoon and went by to help with the other students, freeing Mrs. Dornberger to give Daniel some special assistance with math.

I had a hunch that our neighbors on Cherry Lane panicked when they saw us moving in, a gang in a hippy car with four rowdy boys and a collie dog. We saw them carefully manicuring their yard on Sunday mornings, back and front. If there ever had been a blade of grass in our backyard, it didn't last long, for the boys played there to their hearts' content and worked on many a project. Sometimes, the boys and I set up our tent in the backyard and pretended we were camping, singing songs around a campfire, roasting marshmallows, and telling stories. The boys set up an Olympic scene at one point, high jumps and all.

I brought home scrap lumber from a building or a demolition site occasionally, along with hammers, nails, and saws from the hardware store for the boys to build things with. They first built a fort behind the garage; then Paul remodeled it to make a pigeon coop. A kind man gave him a group of homing pigeons, which he enjoyed caring for. But one night, someone left the cage open, and the birds flew away—all except one mama who stayed with her eggs. Even though all the others abandoned her, she remained, following her maternal instinct. This experience impressed the boys greatly.

Paul decided to establish a worm farm in the backyard, from which he planned to make a lot of money selling fish bait. He built the worm bed with scrap lumber and purchased the "seed" worms. Alas, a torrential downpour came, lasting two or three days, and at the end of the deluge, the worms had all floated away. The worm farm was out of business indefinitely.

The sailboat was another of Paul's projects. He bought an old vessel from a friend and spent weeks on its rehab. He sanded, painted, and sealed it and made sails from old sheets, using my sewing machine.

Finally, the day came when he could realize the results of his dedicated efforts. We towed it to the dock at Lake Austin, at the end of Cherry Lane and launched it. I sat on the dock as Paul and a buddy sailed it out quite far. So far, so good. Suddenly, a strong wind came along and bent the mast as if it were a wet noodle. Over it went, hanging into the water. I waved a passing speedboat and dispatched the driver to rescue the downhearted sailor and his boat.

None of these failures appeared to discourage Paul. Perhaps they were simply good preparation for dealing with future disappointments.

Our dog Taj had several litters of adorable and healthy puppies before we had her spayed. When it was time for her to deliver her last litter, she disappeared, and we couldn't find her. Worried, we searched the neighborhood and covered a field nearby, calling her name. The next day, a neighbor came to report that he had heard the puppies crying underneath his window the night before. All the while, she had been behind the shrubbery, giving birth. The boys were deeply impressed by her maternal love and care for her pups.

One morning, after my boss and his wife Ellen and their children had joined us for a cookout in our backyard the previous evening, we noticed a gap in the neighbors' Venetian blind. We surmised that they had pulled it apart to peek at us the night before.

I was often a little embarrassed by our noisiness, wondering what they thought of us. I was sure that they could hear our quarrelling. Then I realized that, while we never heard them quarrel, we never heard them laugh either.

When we returned one Sunday night from a camping trip, we saw that the neighbors had placed plastic strips into the chain link fence, creating more privacy for themselves. I figured they were tired of looking at all the mess next door. The boys promptly took down the pigeon coop and used the lumber to make a tree house.

On Saturdays, we cleaned house while Thomas was at the library. I made a list of what needed to be done and divided it by four. Whoever signed up first got the best picks, so that the last one to sign up got to clean the bathroom.

A blank line on the list was for any task that anyone could sign up for that they saw needed doing The first time Paul volunteered for something in that spot, I said, when it was completed, "Oh, Paul, you don't know how pleased I am. I've been waiting for four years to get this done." After that, every Saturday, he would ask, "Mom, do you have anything that's been waiting for four years?"

Thomas and the boys often went to the "Y" to play basketball on Saturday after lunch and chores were completed.

Mark, Paul, and Justus all had paper routes at one time or another while Daniel did yards in the neighborhood. I helped fold and bag the papers when the manager was late with the delivery, drove the route on a rainy day, and filled in when one of our paperboys was off at camp. Thomas helped with it occasionally. Collecting the money was the worst part—some people had moved away, "didn't have the correct change," or weren't home. Sure, I resented it sometimes, as I pulled the red wagon, loaded with papers, up and down the hills in the hot summer afternoons. But what choice did I have?

Children are brilliant in the way they modify and adjust their behavior in order to survive a chaotic home life, and their behaviors provide the benefit of balance in the family. The four childhood survival behaviors have been identified as Scapegoat, Hero, Lost Child, and Mascot. The trouble starts when, as adults, not realizing that we no longer need these old behaviors, we continue the archaic roles in new relationships. That's how we recreate the same unsatisfactory relationship repeatedly.

Someone once commented to me, "Peggy, your boys are all so different," and I replied, "Naturally. A family needs only one Hero, one Scapegoat, one Lost Child, and one Mascot, and I have one of each."

While the oldest child is usually the Hero, Mark became the Scapegoat instead. I have some idea about how he was set up early for this role, but who is to say? It took only a few failures for him to assume the role of "Screw-up," and the family's comments and expectations reinforced his view of himself, creating a vicious cycle. There have been many times when I've watched, painfully, as he set himself up for blame and criticism. It was unconscious on his part, of course, though it was apparent to others. I believe the family short-changed Mark in some ways, and I would give years off my life to make it different for him.

Outside the family, Mark showed strong leadership skills. He was the president of the student council as a high school senior, took a big part in the city's Think Trees campaign, and is the main person who introduced soccer to the City of Austin.

While Mark was in college, I advised him to become an elementary school teacher because he was so good with children. Now, he is an excellent teacher of deaf children in the public schools and has a keen sense of social justice. I often remind him that he is just as much a hero as Paul.

Paul, who assumed the Hero role that Mark missed out on, was eagerly helpful and handy in fixing things, so it was easy to praise him. He admits that for all the times when Mark got into trouble, he was more clever at not getting caught. After earning a master's in Range Management at Texas A&M, he worked in South America with the King Ranch of Texas for a while and now manages a large Florida farm for them. He is highly regarded by the company.

Daniel, our loving Lost Child, didn't pick up on information as normal people do and often was lost in a group conversation or while watching TV. I believe that when he didn't understand what was going on and didn't know to ask questions, he simply tuned out and missed even more. Dan works slavishly at his lawn and tree service, and his customers love him. He is one of the most loving people I know, and I have never known him to say or do a mean thing to anyone. On a recent outing at the beach with his brothers, Dan wrote in the sand, "I love everybody."

Justus was our delightfully entertaining, hyperactive Family Mascot who kept the family and others entertained. I enrolled in a creative dramatics course for children at the University of Texas when Justus was five and took him with me for the Saturday workshops. He was by far the most creative and uninhibited of all the children. I had hoped he would become a professional clown or some other kind of enterainer. He now works at a coffee company in Eugene, Oregon; plays music; and works lovingly with children at his church. After many years of smoking marijuana and drinking, he has been in recovery for seven years with the help of Alcoholics Anonymous.

This was a vital and interesting time to be involved in a Black college and a Black church. We were the only white members of Wesley United Methodist, the church that we visited that first Sunday with Dr. and Mrs. King. We understood that the only way to truly be involved in the Black community was through the church. We felt welcome as White liberals but, not wanting our presence simply to be a token, we did all we could to understand and connect with the Black experience. I read everything I could get my hands on about all the issues.

We had few White friends in those days, so the church and college became our community. Thomas worked two summers for the University YMCA on a project in a small pocket of impoverished Black families. During those weeks, we visited almost every Black church in town and were received graciously.

There was one wee church that left a deep impression with me. The service was what one might call "primitive," but I called it beautiful. There was an antiphonal style to the service, with the preacher saying a few words and the tiny congregation responding with the same lines each time. They welcomed us over and over and insisted we come again.

I became more acutely aware and sensitive to racial prejudice. We parked next to a car with several Black children in it one day. The children called out to our boys, "Hey, niggers!" My heart ached for them as I imagined how many times they themselves had been called that very thing.

I looked over a table of marked-down LP records one day at the grocery store near the college. A young Black man about college age was looking at the same display and, not knowing whether he was a student whom I should recognize, I spoke to him.

"Can you tell me which of these records might be good to buy? I've been out of the country for a while," I asked.

Suddenly, he shifted into an act reminiscent of old-time Blacks and in an obsequious, overly polite manner explained that he just wouldn't have any idea. I thought about how far some had come and how far others still had to go.

When Thomas received his fall contract at the end of the spring semester, it was the same as the previous year—$5,000, gross. Thomas was ready to look for another job and move on, but I put my foot down.

"We're not moving!" I declared. "You go in and ask for more money!" He did so and received a small increase.

Carnegie Mellon University invited Thomas to participate in a six-week program for the summer of 1966 to learn teaching methods most effective for minorities. The boys and I drove to Georgia to stay with my parents on the farm, as we did for several future summers. The microbus had little power and could get up to 55 miles per hour if we had a good tail wind, and we camped and picnicked along the way because we had little money.

The boys had a fine time on the farm for seven weeks. They watched the piglets and calves being born and the hay being baled, learned to shell peas, shuck corn, drive the tractor, and eat corn on the cob, black-eyed peas, and a lot of fried fish and chicken. They stalked several sows that were due to deliver babies, growing more and more excited and impatient until, finally, the birthing began. Mark came running in, calling, "Mama, she's letting them out!" Later, he ran back in, shouting, "She's eating all those plastic bags they came in!"

There was an abandoned yellow school bus in back by the barn that Uncle Hoke had used for hauling neighborhood people to church. The boys played for many hours there and in the hayloft with their cousins. I sometimes took them into town to swim rather than let them get in the pond that was now polluted and covered with algae. Our dear collie Taj, named after the Taj Mahal, enjoyed being on the farm as well, but she didn't like riding in the car. It apparently made her carsick, and she drooled the whole way and wouldn't eat.

Celebration!

The laundry was piled up high the day I decided to drive into town and do it at a Laundromat instead of using the wringer washing machine in the pump house. When I arrived, however, I saw the sign reading "Whites only" and knew it didn't mean "white clothes." I took the wash back to the farm and did it the hard way. I'm not sure that I proved anything that day except that I was a glutton for punishment.

My interactions with my mother were strained because we disagreed about the Civil Rights Movement, and she was still angry about my having brought disapproval upon myself and, thus, upon her. Again, she thought it was all about her. Mama made disparaging comments to me and cut me down a lot, and I often got defensive. I know that having us all there for such a length of time was hard on her.

Daddy disagreed with me also but wasn't vicious about it.

During those years, I had considerable conflict with my family about the Vietnam War and racial issues. My brothers taunted me, and I reacted. I learned, eventually, to smile in a subtle manner and let their comments float by.

The "Savannah folks" complained that I apparently had changed, that I wasn't the sweet girl I used to be. Mama reported that Uncle Jack asked her, "What's happened to Peggy?"

I said to my parents, "I haven't changed at all; it's you that have changed. You taught me brotherhood, and now that you are forced to face the very principles you taught me, it's a different matter."

Looking back, I realize that I had hurt them by my arrogance and superior attitude. I forgot that God loves everyone equally. It was especially true years later, after reading the book *Brother to a Dragonfly* by William Campbell, a Baptist preacher in Mississippi. Will had been active in the Civil Rights Movement and quite liberal in his politics until the day his friend P.D. challenged his Christian faith. P.D. named two acquaintances who were both known to be illegitimate and asked Will, "Which of those two bastards does God love most?"

"Now, sitting in the presence of two of the most troubled men I have ever known, I was about to receive the most enlightening theological lesson I had ever had in my life. Not from Louisiana College, Tulane, Wake Forest, or Yale University Divinity School. But sitting here, in a heavily mortgaged house in Fairhope, Alabama, with P.D. East and Joseph Lee Campbell (Will's brother) as teachers. And me as pupil."

Through P.D.'s confrontation, Will realized that God loves everyone just the same, even those on the other side of the issues. He wrote:

"My calls had been to the Department of Justice, to the American Civil Liberties Union, and to a lawyer friend in Nashville. I had talked of the death of my friend as being a travesty of justice, as a complete breakdown of law and order, as a violation of Federal and State law. I had used words like redneck, backwoods, wool hat, cracker, Kluxer, ignoramus, and many others. I had studied sociology, psychology, and social ethics and was speaking and thinking in those concepts. I had also studied New Testament theology.

"In a few minutes, suddenly everything became clear. Everything. It was a revelation. The glow of the malt, which we were well into by then, seemed to illuminate and intensify it. I walked across the room and opened the blind, staring directly into the glare of the street light. I began to whimper. But the crying was interspersed with laughter. It was a strange experience. I remember trying to sort out the sadness and the joy, just what was I crying for and what was I laughing for. Then this too, became clear.

"I was laughing at myself, at 20 years of a ministry which had become, without my realizing it, a ministry of liberal sophistication...looking to government to make and verify and authenticate our morality, of worshiping at the shrine of enlightenment and academia, of making an idol of the Supreme Court, a theology of law and order, and of denying not only the faith I professed to hold but my history and my people....I had never considered myself a liberal. I didn't think in those terms. But that was the camp in which I had pitched my tent. Now I was not so sure."

He said to P.D. later, "Damned if you ain't made a Christian out of me. And I'm not sure I can stand it."

Will Campbell's story moved me and in it, I could see myself as having been self-righteous and condescending. That was the beginning of my moderation from being an morally superior, knee-jerk liberal to being more of a thinking liberal with more compassion for those whose experience is different.

Thomas came to the farm at the end of his course at Carnegie. We planned to drive to Minnesota to see his parents and then home to Austin. I suppose it was out of fear that he reacted so violently when he discovered that the younger brother of a high school classmate had come to the farm to visit me.

This young man had admired my work in Cuba and through the years had tried to emulate it through his own missionary activities. There certainly was nothing about him that I found attractive; I was simply being a friend.

Thomas harassed me for three days and grabbed me and hurt my arm.

Finally, I declared, "I'm not hearing any more of this. Here is what you are to do. Get in the car right now, go straight into town, stop at a store, and get a handful of change. Then go to a pay phone, and talk this over with your dad!"

He didn't go into town, but he didn't mention the issue again. Perhaps he began to see it through his dear father's eyes. In a few minutes, he took out the vacuum cleaner and began to clean the floor. But he didn't acknowledge the abuse or express remorse.

Carnegie invited Thomas to return for the fall semester on the same grant; and when he checked with me about it, I approved. He had already decided to leave the ministry for good and began talking about a Ph.D. program in the field of sociology.

His master's in seminary had been in Social Ethics, so this was his field of interest.

Thomas argued that the work at Carnegie would be counted toward a Ph.D. He reasoned that the advanced degree would be like a union card, insuring employment as a teacher and providing a good income. With the final degree, he said, we would have no financial problems, and he could put the boys through college. He hadn't noticed the many Ph.D.s in Austin who drove taxicabs and flipped hamburgers for a living.

I was opposed to the Ph.D. because we had already been in school for so long and I was running on empty. I often complained that I feared life would be over before we even got around to living it, but Thomas accused me of not cooperating.

I knew that there was no stopping him, as he appeared to need the Ph.D. as a drowning person needs a breath of air. I knew that if I forced him to make a choice between the family and the doctorate, he would choose the degree and that I couldn't support myself and the children with a bachelor's degree in religion. I also knew it would take him forever to finish it without my help, if he ever did get it done.

In reality, I had no say in the matter. As it turned out, the work at Carnegie did not count, and neither did any of his work at Boston because he had been registered at the School of Theology instead of the regular graduate school.

The boys and I got through the fall semester with Daniel and the other boys in school and Justus in nursery for the morning. I worked at the college in the mornings and peddled encyclopedias some evenings, leaving the boys with a sitter.

In December, while Thomas was still at Carnegie, I purchased a new dress to wear to a dinner given for World Book sales representatives. It was red and, according to the newer styles, reached slightly above the knee but was in no way provocative. When Thomas saw it and learned that I had worn it to a party, he caused a big fuss.

Did I look so good in it that I couldn't have other men see me wearing it? That was enough. Raising my voice, I declared, "I'm sick of your self-centeredness, your thoughtlessness, your insensitivity, your lack of gratitude, and your verbal abuse; but most of all, I'm sick of your rotten disposition!"

He said not a word and after that and calmed down noticeably for a while.

I made several attempts to get us into marriage counseling during our years in Austin, with negative results. Once, when we were in the office of a social worker at Child and Family Services, Thomas declared that he did not have the time for this and that we couldn't afford it.

I was begging for help when I said to the social worker, "I'm afraid I'm going to have a nervous breakdown."

Thomas looked at her and complained, "She keeps threatening me with that," and that was the end of counseling.

Thomas began looking into graduate schools as soon as he began teaching the second semester. The Sociology Department turned him down, but he had received a Ford Foundation grant to study and needed to find some program that would take him.

Desperate, he began talking about moving back to Boston where he had been dropped from their program earlier. When I questioned the rationality of this, he reasoned that because the dean at Boston had given him a favorable recommendation for the Mission Board, he possibly would let him back into the doctoral program.

But once again I declared, "We're not moving!"

The Journalism Department accepted Thomas, finally; he made top grades there and was admitted into journalism's equivalent of Phi Beta Kappa. It would take us five long years.

When I had no choice but to endure,
I dug deep and found resources of strength
I never would have imagined were there.

CHAPTER TWELVE

LIFE IN AUSTIN, 1971-1975

The Davidsons, a family with four children—three boys and one girl-- were among our few white friends. The oldest was Mark, three years older than our Mark, who became a good friend and role model for our Mark. Bob was the student minister for the Presbyterian Student Center at the University of Texas, and Marilyn, a gifted musician, taught piano. We became close friends, having much in common, theologically, politically, and socio-economically.

When they called on an occasional Saturday morning to suggest that we meet them at Bastrop State Park for a cookout, we hurried with our cleaning, packed up, and headed out. The boys had wonderful times playing as we adults prepared the food, engaged in many fine discussions, and laughed a lot. Marilyn and Bob both had a great sense of humor.

The Davidsons persuaded us to join them one summer at one of their favorite places—a Presbyterian conference center in the desert west of Santa Fe, called Ghost Ranch. We attended the family conference while camping at the grounds there with other families.

I was busy getting the boys in line one afternoon and was late for the meeting, which was in a building on the mesa. I ran so fast up the hill that by the time I entered the room and took my seat, I was totally winded and gasping for breath.

The guy next to me leaned over and whispered, not so softly, "I'd give you mouth-to-mouth resuscitation, but I'm afraid I'd become emotionally involved!"

The group broke up in hearty laughter.

Toward the end of the week, we were each asked to write something that we felt deeply about our relationship and pass

it to the facilitator. I wrote, "I feel and believe that I do not have the right to have any needs of my own."

When my concern was read aloud, people were stunned—all except Thomas. Even after I owned it as mine, he did not seem to hear it.

Thomas was in the middle of his Ph.D. program by this time, and I was in the middle of typing, revising, editing, and retyping—on a portable typewriter. We learned that he was required to write a Master's thesis in addition to the dissertation as part of the Ph.D. program.

There were times when, if we did something that I especially enjoyed, such as going to the beach or making love, Thomas reminded me that we were doing it mostly for my benefit.

"Well, then, let's not do it," I would say sarcastically. "I'm not worth it!"

We traveled and camped with the Davidsons all over the Southwest. When the children got a little older, their daughter did not care to be among those seven boys, so she stayed with the neighbors while the neighbors' son came along with us. Now we had eight long-legged, hollow-legged, active boys in our party. When the oldest began to drive, we put all of them into one station wagon, and we adults rode together in the other vehicle, a very fine plan.

We usually stopped at a grocery store shortly before lunchtime to purchase food for the rest of the day and looked for a rest area along the highway. Marilyn and I put lunch out—usually milk, punch, sandwiches, and fruit or salad—and called the boys to come. Ignoring us, they continued to play until we announced, "We're packing up!" We eventually learned to call to them as soon as we had everything on the table, "Okay, we're ready to pack up," and they came running.

One of the things we enjoyed in Austin was hosting international students whom we had in our home often. Thomas was keenly interested in people from other countries and cultures and often brought home newly discovered folks, like stray cats. One such person was a Chinese man whose name I have forgotten. Thomas met this man on Chinese New Year at the University of Texas campus and brought him home to eat with us that evening, much to my own delight.

This man, as a boy, had been a student at the same Methodist-Anglo Chinese Boys' School where we worked in Singapore. When his father died, he had to drop out of school to help support his family. He married and had a family but continued studying on his own.

At age 55, after working long enough to draw retirement pay, he left his house and all his savings with his wife and came to America to complete his education. He somehow got into the University of Texas as a freshman without so much as high school diploma. He studied hard while holding a part-time job and left school after his junior year in order to work long enough to draw social security. He was one of the most resourceful people I ever knew.

After his class work was complete at the end of spring semester in 1970, Thomas began his research. Some of the information he needed was on microfilm at the library. When he discovered that, for $1,000, he could purchase his own set of the film, making the research easier, he proposed that we borrow the money and acquire it. I responded, with bitter sarcasm, "I have a better idea. Why don't we just sell the children? Then you could buy all the microfilm you need!" That was all that needed to be said.

For his research, Thomas needed need to travel, which meant that he would not be working at all during the summer. It seemed impractical for me to work and hire someone else to provide childcare, so in March I began looking for a situation in which I could work and keep the boys with me.

Thomas was doubtful. "You'll never find anyone who'll hire you with four boys to look after," he predicted.

By a surprising fluke, my friend Sue Forster happened to mention that she was going to work at a Y.M.C.A. camp for the summer and take her three boys. Her husband was working on his dissertation as well. Storer Camp is located near Napoleon, Michigan, and is owned and operated by the Y.M.C.A. in Toledo, Ohio. I could hardly believe Sue's luck.

I wrote the director a long letter that day stating all my qualifications and was disappointed to learn that all the positions had been filled. Now it appeared that we would have to go on welfare for the summer unless I could find something to do at home.

Then, one Sunday night, a call came from Ann Arbor, Michigan. It was Judy Mohr, the director of the girls' part of the camp. She said that one of the unit directors she had hired had dropped out and asked if I could still take the job. I almost jumped through the phone as I responded in the affirmative. Judy told us later that the trustees almost fainted when she told them that she had hired two women as village directors and that, between us, we were bringing seven children.

I was working at the University for the dean of the School of Journalism by this time. I gave my resignation for the summer, and we began to prepare for our trip, gathering sleeping bags, footlockers, and bug spray.

Sue and I took senior lifesaving in preparation for our work as unit directors. Four days before our departure, I was practicing the "fireman's" dive at the community pool. This dive requires one to jump into the water feet first, using a scissor kick as one reaches the water, in order to keep the head above the water and not lose sight of the drowning victim. The water was too shallow where I dove in, and I hit the bottom with my foot and sprained it badly.

I was in a dilemma now. What if the thing was broken and we couldn't go to camp? I soaked it in cold water, wrapped it in ice, and carried on. I feared that if I went to the doctor, we might find that it was broken, and there was no way I could not do the camp job. I limped on that foot for the whole summer; and once back home, it finally quit hurting, and I learned that it had not been broken after all. Years later, I had surgery on that foot.

Mark, Daniel, and Paul participated in the first two-week session of camp. Mark went on a canoe trip in the Upper Peninsula, and Paul went to Primitive Camp for the second two-week session. During that summer, Mark also participated in the ranch program and a backpacking trip in the mountains of New Hampshire.

After having a few rough days on the boys' side of the lake, Daniel adjusted and stayed for the first two-week session, then came to the girls' side to be with Justus and me. The counselors on the girls' side found the perfect spot for him—helping with the horses and cleaning the barn and corral—and they grew to adore him. At the closing ceremonies at the end of the summer, he received a special award for his diligence and sweet personality.

Justus was too young for the program, so he hung out with Judy Mohr's husband Jim, who took him and Sue's youngest boy fishing and swimming almost every day.

The older boys were in camping programs the entire summer, worth hundreds of dollars, and I was paid a salary besides. What a deal. All the boys thrived and grew in self-confidence, sensitivity, and maturity. In all, Mark was part of the camp program for five straight summers, either as a camper or as staff. Paul went for four summers, taking part in the ranch program, the primitive camping program, a canoe trip, and work on the maintenance crew.

Sue and I made a great effort to be hired for the following summer, but the trustees nixed it because hiring us with all those kids was too expensive. I said that I would do the job without pay in order to give the boys another summer there, but they didn't take me up on it.

I drove with the younger boys to Georgia that next summer to spend time with my parents while Thomas did more research for his dissertation. Paul had saved some money to pay for camp and planned to take a bus from Georgia to Michigan. But Paul, the two younger boys and I were in a serious wreck on the way to the bus, and Paul ended up in the hospital with a head injury. He had to wait to attend camp the following summer.

We put Justus on the bus when he was 12 and old enough to go as a camper and gave him detailed instructions and cautions about the trip. Our dear friend Ann Alexander met him at the bus station in Toledo and drove him to camp. During the session, Justus, such a daredevil, achieved the honor of having jumped off the high tower into the lake a record number of times. He had sprained his neck by the end, though, and had to take a plane home, wearing a neck brace. Ann fetched him from camp and put him on the plane.

Daniel had a young teacher in sixth grade that was new to Special Education and a little high-strung. At one point, the two of them began to clash, and they became totally frustrated with each other.

Daniel was a passive, loving child and well behaved in a classroom with other students who were hyperactive, disruptive, and easily distracted. He could lose it, however, when unduly stressed and frustrated.

Another student annoyed Daniel for days until finally, one day while in line for lunch, right in front of the principal's office, the kid stomped on Daniel's foot. Daniel blew up. He really lost it this time.

The principal asked us to remove Daniel from school, and we did. We placed him in Hill School, which was a good experience for him as it turned out.

Daniel had unfinished business at the old school, however. He was so desperate for his teacher's approval that he kept running away from the new school, which was a great distance away, and showing up in his old classroom. He escaped from the house once before dawn and ended up miles and miles from home, lost and looking for his teacher's residence and for the acceptance he hoped to find there.

He was desperate when we reached him, but not so desperate that he hadn't accumulated a pocketful of money on the way by gathering discarded glass bottles and turning them in for cash.

Daniel settled down after several stressful weeks and, with the excellent help and support of Dr. Jack Day, child psychiatrist, and the counselors at the new school, he thrived.

With trust and trepidation, we put Daniel into a two-week program that summer at Sports Country, a camp in the Hill Country. We hoped he was stable enough to be away from home that long. At the end-of-camp graduation, we enjoyed seeing the boys demonstrate their skills and receive various awards. The presentation for the Outstanding Camper Award came at the end of the program. As the director told what this award stood for and described the camper who had been chosen to receive it, I leaned over to the person next to me and whispered, "I know he's not talking about my camper!" Then I heard the words, "And this year's award for the outstanding camper goes to—Daniel Grose!" What a victory that was for us all. I believe Daniel still has that trophy.

The boys and I made many improvements to the place during the eight years that we lived on Cherry Lane. We painted the kitchen a chili red on the wainscoting with harvest gold on the wall and the kitchen cabinets, and my artistic neighbor painted sunflowers on the cabinet doors. I bought some large sombreros and painted them, too, and hung them on the wall. We also painted the exterior siding an olive gold and the trim off-white; but first, we had to scrape and sand the many layers of peeling paint on the trim. I had new window screens and window boxes made, painted them off-white, and put red geraniums in the boxes. I learned to float, tape, and plaster sheetrock as well as any professional—maybe better, because it was my house and I took more care with it. I owe a lot of thanks to the patient folks at the hardware store where I bought materials and received instructions.

I said I would put in a lawn in the front if it killed me, and it almost did. I had a dump-truck load of dirt hauled in, but it was damp and difficult to spread, taking me weeks to get it completed.

Celebration!

I "liberated" some camshafts from foreign cars from Gene's scrap yard to make into candleholders, spray painting them gold. They had decorative ridges on them that American cars don't have, and I could see the possibilities while Gene couldn't picture it. I helped myself to some rims as well to make into footstools, painted them gold, and made cushions to fit. A visitor looking around our living room asked, "Thomas, how is your car running?"

There was a stump at the front corner of the house where a tree had been cut down for being too close to the foundation, I suppose. I set my mind to removing that eyesore and purchased a product that was supposed to eat away the wood and make it soft enough to dig out. It helped some, but there was still work to be done.

I hacked at it for a while with an axe, then devised better a plan. I took a metal garbage can, punched holes in it with an ice pick, and poured some lighter fluid on the stump. I set fire to it and put the garbage can over it to keep from burning down the house. It worked. I was able to dig out the rest, once it cooled down, and put in some good soil. Now I was rid of the eyesore and able to plant a very nice, small Japanese yew tree, which thrives to this day.

In the summer of '72, while Thomas was doing community work in a mostly-Black neighborhood, he met a young Black man who was lifeguard at the pool. His white girlfriend was pregnant, and they wanted to get married, but her parents objected violently because of racial and religious differences. The date was set for the ceremony to take place on a pretty hillside out of town, and Thomas was to perform the rites.

But in order to prevent the marriage, the parents intervened and attempted to have the young woman committed to a mental hospital.

Two weeks later, on a Sunday afternoon, the couple called and said they wanted to have the service at our house that afternoon. The house was a mess, the front yard was torn up with grass planting, and mud had been tracked into the house. I had exactly two hours to spruce things up. The wedding cake came out of the freezer, and the table was set for refreshments by the time guests arrived. It was a lovely time, and we remained friends with this couple for a long time.

By the summer of '72, Thomas had completed his research and was ready to write the dissertation.

I announced the following plan: "This is the last summer we are going to spend on this project. We are going to bear down and complete this thing. It's now or never!"

The two older boys were in camp, so Thomas and I zeroed in to finish the writing. He wrote a few pages while I typed, revised, edited, and retyped. Then one of us took whatever was finished to his supervising professor for approval or suggested changes. We worked all morning, stopped for lunch, worked until suppertime, and then took the two younger boys and a picnic to the park to play tennis and swim until the pool closed.

We completed the dissertation in late August, in time for him to have his Ph.D. for the fall semester. It was late afternoon when Thomas returned from submitting the finished product, signatures and all. We planned to leave town immediately to drive to Georgia, and I was packed when he returned from the campus.

"I'll never forget what you have done for me," he said, as we put the bags into the trunk of the car.

At last, that magic point in time has come when I am appreciated and will be treated accordingly, I thought.

It was not to be. The patterns were too entrenched; and when I finally left the marriage a few years later, he told me that nothing I had done counted and that there would be no rewards. I recalled his remark recently when reading James Hollis' book *Finding Meaning in the Second Half of Life.* In the book, Hollis recalls the story of Job, who complained to God about how he was being mistreated after having been totally faithful and having done nothing to deserve such misfortune. And God replied,

Celebration!

"We never had any deal!" I had been operating under the same fantasy as Job.

Thomas received a nice raise at Huston-Tillotson College; and the next year, with a larger paycheck, we bought a roomier, more modern house just three doors from the school where Justus would be in fourth grade. I was thrilled with this house.

Thomas insisted that I get a master's degree of my own, which I appreciate.

After we moved into the new house, I took nine hours of undergraduate credits as a prerequisite for graduate school and studied for the Graduate Record Exam, another prerequisite.

My score was not impressive, but my supervisor recommended me, based upon the finding that the older-than-average student usually did better than the average younger one. I entered the master's program at the University in the field of Organizational Communication with a minor emphasis in Management. I also took statistics and a class in Public Relations.

Expect a miracle!

CHAPTER THIRTEEN

KERRVILLE

Thomas soon began looking for a higher-paying job; and in the summer of 1975, he landed the position of academic dean at a college in Kerrville, Texas, in the Hill Country.

We leased out our pretty house in Austin and moved into a small, white '40s-style frame house on campus, without central heat and air and not nearly as nice as the house we were leaving behind. There was nothing modern about this house; but we paid low rent, our utilities were subsidized, and we had the use of all the facilities on campus.

When we visited the college and city of Kerrville during the summer before taking the job, I happened to see an article in the local paper about the monthly meeting of The Methodist Women. It was on the front page of the life section and reported on those who had participated in the program and who served refreshments.

I felt as if I were falling into a deep, dark hole. What did Kerrville have to offer me? Just about the time that my two oldest children were in college and Thomas had his degree, and when I had thought it was now my turn to do my "thing," here I was in what seemed to me an outpost.

Kerrville was good to me, as it turned out. One afternoon, while conferring with Dan's teachers about his program, I saw a poster on the wall with a picture of a huge sunflower growing out of the ground. The caption underneath read, "Bloom where you are planted;" and knowing the message was for me, I got busy.

The wife of the former college president held a welcoming luncheon in my honor at the country club, so I knew that if I wished, I could play tennis in the mornings with the "right" people and bridge in the afternoons at the "right" places. I had better things to do, however; I just didn't know what they would be.

I had to complete my thesis, for one thing. I made a trip into Austin monthly to see my supervisor and visit friends, returning to Kerrville each time, renewed. I heard of a good book, a good movie, and some refreshing thoughts while in town.

I stayed overnight with some friends on one of my trips to Austin and needed to call Thomas at home in Kerrville. I placed the call, telling the operator, "I am Peggy, and I wish to place a collect call to (830) 257____."

She came back on the line in a few moments and announced, "Your party wants to know, 'Peggy who?'"

I asked Thomas, when I arrived home, "Who is the person named *'Peggy'* who was most likely to call you at your *home, late in the evening, collect?*"

He explained that he had received an application for a teaching position from a woman named "Peggy" and thought it may be her.

I had long known where I stood, but this confirmed it, once and for all.

In February of 1976 at age 42, I attended a weeklong workshop farther up in the Hill Country at Mo Ranch, a Presbyterian conference center that had once been a working ranch. The workshop was called "Getting in Touch with Your Feelings." These were the "touchy-feely" days of the '70s.

The sessions began on Sunday evening, and on Thursday, the group facilitator instructed each of us to close our eyes and imagine ourselves as a rose bush.

I saw what had once been a rose bush, standing in dry, cracked earth, without one green leaf or a single red petal. Twenty-two years earlier, I had been Miss LaGrange College, a runner-up in the Miss Georgia Pageant, listed in *Who's Who in Colleges and Universities*, and maid of honor in the May Court. Now I

was nothing but a dried-up rose bush, a shattering image. I had known for a long time that I was hurting but hadn't realized that I was dying.

I knew that I would have to leave my marriage; and when I mentioned it to a dowdy woman in her 50s, she advised, "Well, have all the fun you can now, honey, because after you're 50, men won't notice you."

That may be true for you, but not necessarily for me, I thought.

Thomas had already informed me, just before we moved from Austin, that he no longer found me attractive because I was getting older.

I had responded, "So? You were never attracted to me in the first place, even when I was young. You never wanted me; you only needed me."

When I was ready to make my move two-and-a-half years later and start a new life and a new career, a male friend, in wide-eyed innocence asked, "Is your age going to be a problem?"

Now I began to wonder, "*Is my life over, just as I was planning its beginning?*"

I arranged and conducted consulting and training for employees at the local bank during the spring of 1976, taught a class in organizational communication for the hospital, became a certified trainer for Parent Effectiveness Training and finished my thesis. I wrote a weekly column for the local newspaper called "Improving Family Harmony," which was well received. I became the director of the community school the next fall, a joint project of the city and school district. I enlisted volunteer teachers for various subjects and scheduled and supervised classes and promoted the program in the community by speaking at civic clubs and putting weekly notices in the newspaper.

One day during our third year in Kerrville, Thomas complained to me, in blaming tones reminiscent of that old "Ring-Around-the-Collar" commercial, that he didn't have any clean white socks. (He had athlete's foot and changed twice a day.)

I said, trying to control my voice, "You have two bachelor's degrees, two master's degrees, and a Ph.D., so I am pretty sure that you can learn to operate the f-----g washing machine!"

And he did.

I applied to be the director of a slim-fitness camp in January of 1977. A company in San Diego owned the camp, using our campus facilities in Kerrville each summer. When I saw the resumé of the woman who got the job, I realized why I wasn't selected, for her credentials were impressive.

I guess she was better on paper than in person, for, one week after camp opened, things began to implode. She had hired her best friend as assistant director, but the two of them soon had a falling out and began to sabotage each other and the camp as a whole. Each was enlisting the campers and staff on her side; the nutritionist quit, as did the nurse and some of the counselors. Some of the campers called their parents to come get them, at the direction of one of the counselors.

Howard Hall, the business manager at the college and the liaison between the camp and its parent office, called the owner Lee Waters. "Lee, you'd better get out here now. Your camp is about to close," he warned.

Lee took the next plane and arrived at about noon on Friday. After firing the director and her assistant, and with his head in his hands Lee asked, "Howard, what am I going to do? I need a director, *now.*"

"Well, there is a woman right here on the campus who applied for the job, but she's teaching summer school," Howard replied.

"Get her down here!" Lee shot back. He offered me the job, which I said I would accept only after talking with the remaining staff and getting a feel for the situation.

I met with the staff members, who were willing to make a new start and to put the program back together, and I accepted. None of us knew that the one counselor had instructed the girls to call their parents to come for them and were shocked when the first of about 30 cars began to arrive—just as I stepped out of the lounge as the newly hired director. Wow, was I in for an interesting weekend.

By the way, Lee took himself to a hotel to get some rest.

I told the staff to carry on with whatever programs they had planned while I talked with these people.

Rumors were flying—the pool was polluted, everyone had food poisoning and skin infections, and the directors were chasing each other with butcher knives. I sat for three days in the shade of a tree, talking with the parents, expressing empathy for their concern, but assuring them that their daughters were safe. Most of them remained for the entire weekend. They sat and observed as we carried on with the program and watched me as I talked with other parents.

A large man wearing a dirty, white T-shirt and gasping for breath barged into the office toward suppertime on Friday and demanded to know where the director was. I informed him that I had just been hired as the new director, but he ignored me. Pressing a button covering a hole in his throat in order to talk, he hissed, "I have a list of all the campers here. I've called the attorney general's office and the sheriff's on his way! I'm going to shut this place down, Lady!"

About two dozen campers had crowded in to watch the excitement by this time.

I figured I'd better employ some of my best reflective listening skills. I listened patiently and replied empathically to him, afraid he would have a heart attack right then and there. I had read that in dealing with terrorists and hostage-takers, the government sends in negotiators who are street savvy, know the language, and are good listeners. And that the longer you listen, the more they'll talk; and the more they talk, the sooner they'll cool down, and that this reduces the chances of bloodshed. That's exactly what I did.

The man's daughter had joined us by now, a young woman whom I discovered later was one instigator of the trouble. Her motive: She wanted out of camp.

Celebration!

The man cooled down finally, as I explained that the situation was being corrected and that the incompetents had been sent packing.

When Lee returned to the campus the next morning, I suggested that he offer to reimburse the parents of any campers who left, and he agreed. It turned out that out of 100 girls, only 20 left, and they probably were the ones who were least motivated anyway.

We were relieved that we had not one lawsuit. Lee sent an assistant from San Diego, and I hired a nurse, nutritionist, and a lifeguard. Overall, we had a pretty good camp, in spite of the fact that the counselors were a pretty incompetent lot.

Lee offered me the job for the next summer, which I accepted, pleased with the opportunity to interview, hire, and train my own staff. With permission from the company, I extended the training period to one entire week, teaching leadership skills, interpersonal communication, and conducting team building among the staff.

It was time for me to make my move to Austin after the close of camp. The school superintendent urged me to continue as the Community School director on a half-time basis, and Lee sincerely wanted me to direct the camp for the third summer, but I had to get on with my life.

Bloom where you are planted.

CHAPTER FOURTEEN

MAKING THE BREAK

Some of my loneliest times were in church, sitting next to my husband and surrounded by hundreds of people, none of whom knew or cared anything about me. Other lonely times were at night when my husband turned away from me on the other side of the bed and went to sleep without a word.

It seemed that it was difficult for him to speak to me in a conversational tone. At times, I suggested to him, "Hey, pretend that I'm a stranger on the street. Speak to me in the same, respectful way, at least."

The pile of resentment grew deeper and deeper, and it seemed I would choke on the loneliness and despair. I felt invisible eventually, as a servant is invisible, needed for her services but not seen as a person. Sometimes, I locked myself in the bathroom, put my arms around myself, and pretended I was being held. Even though I had been pregnant four times, whenever I saw a pregnant woman, my heart ached from the thought that her husband found her sexually attractive. From the way other men looked at me, I knew I was attractive, so why wasn't I attractive to my own husband? More than once, after failing to get Thomas' attention, I said to him, "I am going to have a romantic love relationship before I die, if not with you, then with someone else!" It made no difference.

My heart ached even more when I read the Theodore Hesburgh quote, "The most important thing a father can do for his children is to love their mother."

I had known for a very long time I would leave the marriage, never realizing how wounded I would be by the end of the relationship. My first therapist diagnosed me as having

Celebration!

Post Traumatic Stress Disorder, and I was later diagnosed with adrenalin exhaustion. (An article I came across read, "...adrenal exhaustion can be caused by emotional tension such as frustration or suppressed rage.") I thought I had to wait for a time when everyone would be in a good place and a time when I could give myself permission to make the break.

Two-and-a-half years after seeing myself as a dried-up rose bush, after Daniel had graduated from high school and Justus from junior high and Thomas was established in his job, it was time. Meanwhile, I had prepared—physically, mentally, and emotionally. I strengthened my support system in Austin, attended workshops on self-image, saw a psychiatrist, got in shape, and had some cosmetic surgery.

It was all behind me when the time came for me to make my move. There was no more grieving to be done.

In March of 1978, without so much as a lead for a new job and with four children yet to educate, Thomas resigned his job as dean of the college, on the spot, because of continued conflict with some of the faculty and staff. In all his spare time from then until his contract ended on the last day of July, he wrote letters and made phone calls, looking for job openings anywhere in the country. He even traveled to Washington, D.C., and the Midwest to inquire about opportunities, putting the expenses on a credit card.

Thomas informed me that he was also seeking a position for me with the same potential employers; but I reminded him, as I had already said, that I was not going with him, but planned to move back to Austin at the end of my girls' camp.

It never occurred to him that I would have any feelings about his resigning the one well-paying job he had ever had after years of study. Or that I would have any problem with packing up, once again, and following him. He made no response when I told him I planned to leave, so I had no reason to believe he would care if I did.

I moved out on August 29, the day of our 24th wedding anniversary and announced that I had leased a house in Austin in my own name. To my surprise and dismay, Thomas came apart and moved into my house in Austin with me. He refused to leave until after the three-month residency requirement that had to be completed before I could file for divorce and force him out.

Those days were cataclysmic, for Thomas had not been listening. He told friends that my move was a total surprise, and he traveled up and down the state, sullying my name among our friends with stories of infidelity and deceit. There are people who were once dear to me who haven't spoken to me since. My studies in relationship dynamics and family systems show that the most crucial and dangerous time in an abusive relationship is when a partner tries to leave the abuser.

I took Justus with me to my friend Jewel's home on the weekends because things were so unpleasant at my house. Dan had already moved back to Kerrville to stay with friends and return to his old job on the campus maintenance crew.

Jewel and her husband, Bob, had a good friend who was recently divorced and whom they wanted me to meet. "Harry is going to flip when he sees you," Jewel predicted.

The four of us went dancing on Saturday nights at a large dance hall patronized by people our age. After being harassed and pushed around during the week at my house, it was healing to have Harry hold me close and waltz me across that big dance floor.

After I filed for divorce and got Thomas out of my house, life became easier; and I thought I could date Harry openly. My attorney had said it would be okay, but it was not so easy. Thomas stalked me and made menacing phone calls until after the divorce was final.

I was deeply sorry that the relationship ended with such bitterness. We had had many fine experiences and had done much good work together. We were equally adventuresome, with many of the same goals, values, and viewpoints. We could have grown old together, enjoying grandchildren and long-time friends. I had gained from those expanding experiences; but my soul was withering, and I had to get away.

I realized that Harry was getting serious and broke up with him after a few weeks because I didn't want to disappoint him more. He was handsome and loving but was not what I wanted.

In the spring of 1979, I became a grandmother when my precious Bretnie was born to Mark and Mary Ruth, and at last we had the girl we had always wanted. I was there for her birth, as well as for my Sean's in 1980, the first of three grandsons, and for Paul and Lenoska's Andrew and Brian who came along a few years later. I have tried to be involved in their lives at every step.

During my 10 years of "singlehood," I was employed as a probation officer, was a counselor/trainer for the National Corrective Training Institute, became a Dale Carnegie Course instructor, a Licensed Chemical Dependency Counselor, and a Licensed Professional Counselor, and helped design Austin's first Assertiveness Training program for the Austin Women's Center. I designed and ran a chemical dependency program for a mental health clinic, worked as a counselor in the county jail, taught communication and public speaking at three colleges, rode a mule to the bottom of the Grand Canyon, took a seven-day canoe trip down the Rio Grande, took the EST training, volunteered for APD's victim services crisis team and for The Center for Attitudinal Healing, and was active in Toastmasters.

Why all the activity? I am interested in so many things and am afraid I'll miss something. Wanting "it all" is not a good thing.

I was the counselor at the Sheriff's Boot Camp for six of the eight years that I worked for the sheriff's office. It was a program for young offenders over 17, much like Marine basic training. I helped set up Texas' first in-jail chemical dependency treatment program and ran that program at the boot camp. I also conducted sessions in interpersonal communication for the cadets and their wives, parents, and girlfriends, held weekend retreats, and oversaw a "Mothers and Their Children" visitation program, in addition to doing a lot of one-to-one counseling.

About 25 of us counselors and nursing staff learned to do auricular acupuncture, a technique whereby one inserts needles into five points in the ear to relieve craving for drugs, including nicotine, and to help one relax and focus. This was part of a plan to ban smoking in the jails and part of drug treatment. Even though many of the cadets had a "thing" about needles, they welcomed the acupuncture.

I installed a ratty old chair with an ottoman in my office, where a person could sit as we talked or rest for 20 minutes while the needles took effect. I wasn't naïve enough not to realize that this often was simply a ruse to get away from the drill instructors and maybe get in a short nap as well.

The cadets stayed in the program anywhere from six months to a year, and I came to know them very well and their parents, too, either from their stories or from meeting the parents over the phone or face-to-face. I saw many family patterns that could explain these kids' involvement in crime—the main one was NO FATHER. Of the fathers who lived in the house and supported their families, most were not engaged with the children. One White kid from an affluent home complained, "When I have a problem, my mother takes me shopping, and my dad pays the bill, but he doesn't talk to me."

I prepared and presented the talk, "The Solution to Crime Begins at Home: For Parents Who Think Their Kids Can't Go Wrong," and a condensed version of it appeared in the *Austin American-Statesman* on the Op-Ed page.

One of my volunteers died in my office, in my presence, as we laughed and joked. A cadet, a marvelous young man who had turned his life around, died outside my office from a blood clot on his brain. These were traumatic events for the cadets and for me.

The time at the boot camp was one of the most significant experiences of my life. How I loved those boys and the few

young women in the program. I often said that if there was only one thing I accomplished, it was that they knew that I cared about them.

I reminded the drill instructors, "You can get these kids down in a front-leaning rest position; you can make them duck walk to the fence and back; you can shave their heads and make them do 25 push ups; but if they don't know you care about them, you're wasting your time."

They ignored me, though; they didn't have much use for counselors except in a crisis; because they thought we were soft. For several years after leaving the program, I occasionally heard a voice in the grocery store, across a parking lot, or in the post office calling, "Hi, Counselor Peggy!" and it would be one of my former cadets.

I became less and less liberal as a result of my many experiences and more and more Libertarian in my views. I began to see that between racism and the welfare system, many people have become dependent. Perhaps Afro-American men were harmed the most. In studying and working in the field of chemical dependency and family systems, I saw how codependent our government is.

The government says, "You're not capable; here, let us do it for you," and this makes for "learned helplessness." In studying management theories, seeing that most people do better when given autonomy and freedom to be responsible and creative, I began to see the wisdom of giving people more responsibility for their lives and holding them accountable. I saw that by doing for people what they can and should do for themselves, they learn to be dependent and to develop low self-esteem. I read that 90 percent of men in prison were born of teenage mothers (read: NO FATHER), which exactly matched my experience working at the boot camp.

I did weekly group counseling sessions at a halfway house for federal offenders with chemical dependency problems. I went into the dining room one evening to find a certain client when another young man walked up and asked, "Where have I seen you before...Oh, you're the chick that was here last week." (I was 65 at the time.)

Another resident sitting nearby, asked, "Do you mind him calling you a 'chick'?"

"Well, it's not very appropriate, but I don't get excited about those things," I answered.

"Do you like being called 'babe'?" he persisted.

I replied that I like it when my husband calls me "Babe."

Just then, another voice called from a far corner, "She's a babe!"

At my age, I loved it!

I picked up the local newspaper one morning in August of 1981 to see the following headlines: "SUICIDE SEEMED LIKE THE ONLY ALTERNATIVE!" and learned that I was the star defendant in an $800,000.00 lawsuit. I was a probation officer for the county, carrying a caseload of 200 felons and had begun revocation proceedings against one of my clients. It was based on several administrative violations. I received a report from the police that my client had been arrested on a DWI charge, and I added that charge to the revocation report.

The client went to jail, where he languished for three weeks without being seen by his court-appointed attorney. It was the sheriff's responsibility to see that he was seen by a lawyer.

A new attorney discovered the error—another man by the same name, same middle initial, but with a different date of birth, was the one who had been arrested for drunken driving—not my client.

It was not my error, but I was one of several people who should have caught it and one of several who signed the revocation papers. In the confusion, my client was released, and the revocation hearing cancelled. The client, with his attorney, went to the media that afternoon and, because I was low on the totem pole and the one delivering the services, I was made the scapegoat.

Celebration!

The media had a field day, flashing the story morning, noon, and night, day after day.

The plaintiff told the reporters stories that made me sound like an ogre, and they printed every word, including his threats of suicide. The reporter kept stating, "Efforts to reach Ms. Gross have been fruitless" or "Ms. Gross could not be reached for comment."

One can guess their mistake: They were using the wrong spelling of my name when looking into the phone book and did not bother to ask my employer how to reach me.

The head of the agency, without even talking to me, promised the reporter, "She will be fired," a defensive move on his part. He did not have a good relationship with the media, and this was an opportunity for them to make us all look bad.

No one from my church called, not even my pastor; and of all my friends, only one person called.

The media kept it up steadily for two weeks until Prince Charles got married.

At last, I thought, looking forward to having a little relief, *The attention is on the royal wedding and not on me.*

I was back in the news a few days later, however. No reporter ever called me to get the other side of the story—that it was not the wrong man in jail; the DWI charge was the only error. I was suspended for two weeks without pay, and this was played up in the news as well. Like snakes that crawl out of their holes during flooding, some of my more "anti-social" clients called in to report their complaints about me.

By a stroke of good luck, I had recently joined the employees' union. When the staff read the story, they went to their files and, to their delight, found my name. They were instrumental in getting me re-instated in my job—although I was put on six months' probation—and in regaining some of the pay I had lost and were supportive all the way.

I was to report back to work on a Monday at the end of my two-week suspension. It happened that I had been scheduled earlier for a regular employee performance review on that very day. I awoke on Sunday morning feeling sorry for myself, dreading the return to work and facing the shame and humiliation. I had planned to attend a special program at the church but decided instead to stay in bed and wallow in a puddle of self-pity. I pulled the cover over my head and tried to go back to sleep.

Abruptly, I said to myself, *You said you were going to the meeting. Now get up and go!*

I did get up and go.

I ran into Don Small while getting coffee on the patio, and he informed me that we had met before. "What a coincidence," I said. "I came across your name and phone number a couple of weeks ago but couldn't remember who you were or how I had come to have your number."

As we sat and drank our coffee, I told him of my situation and how I dreaded the next day. "I think I'd rather just go in and submit my resignation," I whined.

"Peggy, you can play the victim in this; and, if you do, they will victimize you," Don said, "Or you can go in there tomorrow, and let them see just what a strong woman you are."

It was as if I had taken an object and turned it to the opposite side, seeing it entirely differently. I let go of self-pity and fear, calling up an arsenal of courage until I actually looked forward to the next morning. I sailed in with a smile that day, greeting everyone and receiving a warm welcome with many good wishes. My performance review went well, with my supervisor giving me higher scores than I would have given myself.

It reminded me of my fear of the snakes in the outhouse and the fear that was based entirely upon what I couldn't see.

I resigned the job and had begun working with the Dale Carnegie Courses by the time we went to court the next spring. Plenty of reporters were there.

Lest it be seen that they were harassing the plaintiff, the Probation Department declined to re-file revocation proceedings

based upon the original administrative violations. The client was arrested later on new charges, however.

The plaintiffs dropped the case against the county commissioners but retained the suit against the Sheriff, the Probation Department, and me personally. During that trial, I repeated these words in my mind:

> **The LORD is my shepherd; I shall not be in want.**
>
> **He makes me lie down in green pastures;**
> **he leads me beside quiet waters,**
>
> **He restores my soul.**
> **He guides me in paths of righteousness**
> **for his name's sake.**
>
> **Even though I walk**
> **through the valley of the shadow of death,**
> **I will fear no evil,**
> **for you are with me;**
> **your rod and your staff,**
> **they comfort me.**
>
> **You prepare a table before me**
> **in the presence of my enemies.**
> **You anoint my head with oil;**
> **my cup overflows.**
>
> **Surely goodness and love will follow me**
> **all the days of my life,**
> **and I will dwell in the house of the LORD**
> **forever.**

We sat through several days of trial until time for the attorneys to make their closing statements. The plaintiff's attorney brought up some issues in his final arguments that had not been mentioned earlier and made accusations that were entirely false.

Peggy S. Grose

I felt angry and frightened at first, but suddenly, I felt a strange calm. I remembered studying a technique called "fogging" whereby, when under attack, one imagines oneself as a fog bank so that the attack meets no resistance.

The department head sitting next to me became agitated and muttered under his breath, "He's a goddamn liar!"

I whispered, "Shh, pretend you're a fog bank." He gave me a strange look.

I had long seen that I was the only person in the courtroom who was on my side, that the Department was not concerned with protecting my credibility, only theirs. But now I realized that I was the most powerful person in the room, that there was no way they could hurt me, and I began to enjoy the party.

I went down the street to get something to eat when the jury went out to deliberate and was on my way back to the courtroom when I saw everyone leaving the building. The judge had issued a "directed verdict" in our favor instead of allowing the jury to decide.

That made big news in the media, who were for the plaintiff, whom they considered the underdog.

We knew the case would be appealed—and it was, with the directed verdict being thrown out. The case went to the Supreme Court, which determined that a jury in Austin should decide the verdict, not a judge.

The county attorney phoned me, as the date for the new trial approached, with the news that the plaintiffs had offered to settle out of court for $5,000.00; he wanted to know my wishes.

"Definitely not," I said. "We're not going to cave in after all this."

The plaintiffs had dropped the case against the sheriff by this time, and now it was just the Department and me.

We were now in court again, four years later. The media had followed and reported every phase of the case meanwhile, running a photo of the plaintiff every time and repeating all the slanderous things he had said about me. I waited for the "other shoe

to drop" for four years, wanting to promote my own consulting business but not wanting my name to become too recognizable until after the case was finished.

We were in session for a week with a full jury but no reporter was in sight. I surmised that by now, they had realized we actually had done the man no wrong. At the end of the week, the judge gave the panel a list of 10 questions for them to answer, including, "Did the defendant, (I) do the client any wrong?", "Does the Department owe him money?" and so on.

All the answers were in our favor, and it was over at last. The judge thanked the jury for serving and commended them on their verdict, saying that important case law had been made that day.

There was no reporter in the courtroom that week, and nothing was mentioned of the trial in the media.

I was told later by a third party that it was said that my documentation saved our hides, but the administrators never gave me credit for it.

Sometimes, we can be thankful for our worst experiences because of the strength and wisdom they teach us, even though we would never want a repeat performance.

Now I could say, "Huh, I got through that in one piece. Okay, world, what else you got?"

***Every challenge I navigated successfully
made me more resilient for the next one.***

CHAPTER FIFTEEN

LOST IN A FOREIGN LAND

Son Paul was working on his master's degree in ranching at Texas A&M University when my brother Gene bought a small ranch in Colombia, South America. Paul took off the fall semester of 1978 to work on this ranch, partly for the adventure and partly to write a ranch plan for academic credit. He had been interested in working in South America since hearing about that part of the world from his first college roommate and had been studying Spanish in preparation for the time he could go there.

He planned to return home in time for Christmas and for the spring semester of school and invited me to go visit him before his time there ran out. I hesitated because of the cost of the trip. But I realized at the last minute that I was passing up an opportunity I might not have again and called Gene to have him make the arrangements. His contact in Colombia was a man in Bogotá, General Juan Rojas, who was retired from the Colombian army. The general spoke fluent English, was prominent in the country, and Gene trusted him to do much of his business in Colombia.

Gene said he would write the general to inform him that I was coming on the given date and would ask him to contact Paul, who would come from *los llanos* (the plains) to meet me in Bogotá.

The ranch, *La Finca Esmeralda* (the Emerald Farm), was 10 miles outside of San Martin and had no phone, but Paul routinely checked with Pepita, the manager at the Hotel Estrelita, for any messages from the general or from home. I felt a little uneasy about getting a letter to the general in time, but Gene said it would cost at least $100 to call on the telephone.

Celebration!

I flew on a Friday morning from Austin to Houston, then to Bogotá, where I arrived at about 9:00 that evening. From what I had heard of the general, I knew that he would be right there at the bottom of the steps to meet me.

When I saw he wasn't there, I knew he had not received Gene's letter and that Paul did not know I was in the country, even.

I found a porter who gave me enough coins to call the general at his house; and no, he was not expecting me but welcomed me enthusiastically. I took a taxi to his house, according to his instructions and grew a little uneasy as we drove quite a ways into what seemed like a business section of town with no private houses.

We stopped, finally, and the driver got out and rang the doorbell at a place that had an expanding grate across the front entrance. All the lights in the house went on suddenly, and I knew we were at the right place. The general came and welcomed me with open arms.

The general, who had never married, lived with his sister Suna, who also was unmarried. The general insisted that I join him in a drink of Scotch and water, which I did although it tasted terrible.

Suna was happy to meet me. She and the general loved Paul, whom they called *"Pablito"* (a term of endearment using the Spanish version of his name); they treated him as their own son whenever he visited them in Bogotá. Suna showed me my room and said lovingly, "This is *Pablito*'s room."

As we sat in the living room with our drinks, the general commented, "You're just in time. *Pablito* ees coming to Bogotá on Sunday."

Alarmed, I asked, "Why?"

"He ees going to return to the United States," he replied.

I had a sinking feeling, for that meant that I wouldn't get to visit him on the ranch.

The general reassured me, "No probleem. En thee morning, we weel telephone *Pablito*, and he weel come to Bogotá to peek you up."

I slept peacefully in *Pablito's* bed.

In the morning, to my dismay, the telephones were out.

The general reassured me again, "No probleem. We weel poot you on the boos." The general put me on the bus at about noon on Saturday. He placed my suitcase on the rack above me, with instructions not to leave my seat nor take my eyes off the suitcase under any circumstances. He brought me a sandwich wrapped in plastic and a warm Coca-Cola™ with the cap still on it and instructed the young nun in the seat ahead of me to get off at Villavicencia, the halfway point, remove the lid from my drink, and otherwise to look after me.

Once in San Martin, I was to go to the Hotel *Estrelita* and find Pepita,. As we pulled out of the station, I recalled Gene's last instructions: "If for some reason Paul can't meet you in Bogotá, don't take the bus; take a taxi."

We rode through some of the most breathtaking scenery I had ever seen, the Andes Mountains. I saw small houses perched on verdant slopes, clinging by their foundations to stay put as plumes of smoke wafted from their chimney tops. I caught an occasional glimpse of a tiny farmer plowing a terraced field and wondered if the people who lived day in and day out in the midst of this beauty were even aware of it. After all, fish are most likely not aware of the water they swim in.

As for me, I was looking out the window at the oncoming traffic, specifically watching for a white four-wheel-drive vehicle driven by a blond, young American man. What if Paul had decided to leave for Bogotá a day early and we were to pass midway? I was rather miserable.

Then a very smelly man with his goat got on and took the one vacant seat—right next to me. At least it was a distraction from my major concern.

We arrived in San Martin after dark.

I got off the bus with my suitcase and began to look for the hotel, unsuccessfully. I walked up and down and inquired of passersby, *"Donde esta el Hotel Estrelita?"* (Where is the

Hotel Estrelita?) I found it, finally, down an alley and behind the bank.

The phone service had been restored during the afternoon, and the general had informed Pepita that I was coming. She was not pleased. I asked her to call a taxi for me; but she said it was impossible, that I had to wait until morning.

"No way!" I said. "Tomorrow will be Sunday!"

So we argued.

I said, *"Ahora. Es muy importante!"* (Now. It is very important.)

But she insisted that it was impossible.

I couldn't understand half of what she was saying because she was talking so fast.

The phone rang about that time. It was the general, who knew that I would be there by now. He informed me that Pepita was right; the roads to the ranch would be too dangerous at night. Besides, all the taxi drivers would be drunk; after all, it was Saturday night.

There I was in the hotel, 10 miles from Paul, who could easily leave early the next day without me. I lay in bed and tried to send him a message by way of mental telepathy: Paul, your mother is in the hotel in San Martin. *Paul, do not leave for Bogotá in the morning without your mother!*

It didn't work.

Pepita called a taxi for me—a Jeep—bright and early the next morning. I exchanged some money at the bank and was on my way, at last. As we rounded a corner, I saw something that looked familiar—a white four-wheel-drive vehicle parked at the curb, and the person at the wheel looked like a young, blond American man. I yelled at the driver in English, "There he is! Stop! Stop!"

The bewildered man slammed on the brakes as I yelled out the window, *"Pablito! Pablito!"*

There he came, with his long stride, asking, "Mom, what are you doing here?"

I had left home on Friday morning, and now it was Sunday on another continent. Crying and laughing at the same time, I told

him of my frustrating journey. I asked him, later, "What did you think when you saw me there on the street of San Martin?"

"All I could think of was getting you off the street because you were attracting so much attention," he replied. "You were so white, had on that makeup, and were making so much noise."

When we arrived a *La Finca Esmeralda*, the six-year-old daughter of the manager assumed, when she saw me, that Paul had brought a wife from town. She ran into the house, broken-hearted. She had planned on being Paul's wife herself.

Paul had intended to leave for Bogotá on Monday, but we stayed on another week at the ranch.

We had many adventures, including an armadillo hunt through some boggy territory, with barking dogs and very nervous armadillos. The armadillo we caught frantically ran into a hole where it was cornered. While the dogs at the entrance, barking wildly, kept it stranded, the men in our party dug in from the opposite end to capture it. I never heard such a melee.

We rejoined our hunting party at another ranch the next evening to eat the roasted catch. It tasted a little like pork, with similar texture. Each afternoon, we visited other ranches, including a neighbor whose 16-year-old daughter obviously was madly in love with Paul.

We left the plains at the end of the next week and made the scenic drive back to Bogotá where we spent a few days with the General and Suna. Then we flew back to the U. S. in time for Christmas.

Just think what I would have missed if I had stayed safely at home.

> **When we are old, we are more likely to regret**
> **those things we missed out on**
> **than the things we did wrong.**

CHAPTER SIXTEEN

CELEBRATION!

Bob Hall was 15 years younger than I, and his lifestyle was completely different from mine, but we had a deep and meaningful relationship.

I met him one day at noon. I was on my way to take a typing test in order to get work with a temporary agency—a depressing prospect. Feeling weary and downhearted, I decided that I would do better with some food in my stomach, and as I walked through the mall toward the cafeteria, I saw my reflection in a store window.

Stunned, I said to myself, *Look at you—you look sad and bedraggled. Now, stand up straight and walk as if you are a princess.* It worked, as I felt better immediately.

Bob was eating with some coworkers when he caught my eye and winked at me, and without thinking, I winked back. As his group got up to leave, I noticed him stalling, pretending to wipe his mouth with his napkin.

He came over and sat down at my table as his friends moved toward the cashier. "I think you're very attractive," he announced.

I don't remember what I said in return, but I didn't exactly reject the overture. He wanted to follow me home, but I declined that offer, setting a date for later in the week.

Like soul mates, we were playful and passionate and so attuned to each other that there were times when I was sure he could read my mind. My brain had a hard time wrapping itself around the fact that here was a man who was willing to drive all the way across town to make love with me while my own husband had not been willing to reach across the bed.

Bob was a good friend to Justus, who was 14 by now and missing his father, who had moved to his home state of Minnesota to be near his parents.

Bob made a Raggedy Ann doll by hand for my granddaughter one Christmas while visiting his parents in Albuquerque, New Mexico, and brought it back on the plane under his arm, unwrapped. Now, there's a man who's secure about his masculinity.

Bob and I dated for about a year and, at one point, talked seriously of marriage. I realized that while I loved him, he was not the man I should marry because of the many differences in lifestyle. He also realized it, later.

Yet, he was a profound thinker and writer, and being with him was an expanding experience, outside my previous lifestyle. It was wonderful to love and be loved, and I was attracted to his masculine energy.

When I announced that I wanted to see what else was out there, he declared that he wasn't willing to stay in town and know that I was dating others. He put in for a transfer to Albuquerque finally.

It was hard to see him go, and neither of us could have predicted that we would support the telephone company and the airlines for two more years as we arranged four-day honeymoons together. Bob still calls about once every 10 years.

For a woman my age, I had more than my share of fun and attention. One of the men I dated was Alex, whom I met at the gym. I was working hard on the stationary bicycle and didn't notice when he mounted the bike next to me.

He made a comment to get my attention and suggested we get something to eat.

"Fine, let me run home, clean up, and meet you there," I said.

"No," he said, "let's just go the way we are."

That's what we did.

During the meal, when he revealed that he had been divorced for three years, I responded, "How has a man as attractive as you remained single for so long?"

His reply, "Well, I'm not very good marriage material," went right over my head; and after I became emotionally involved with him, I discovered he was right.

When I speak to Al-Anon groups, someone in the audience usually asks how to avoid making the same mistaken choices repeatedly. I tell them this story and add, "There are always indications, warning signs, if only we are willing to see them. If you're looking for someone different from the one you've had, and the one you're with seems familiar, run! And if you're looking for someone who dances a different dance, change your own dance."

As I was nearing my 50th birthday, I recalled those warnings that suggested that my life was about to be over—the dowdy woman who warned that, after 50, men wouldn't notice me and the man who had asked if my age would be a problem. Now I had to decide whether to mourn the end of my life or celebrate a new beginning.

I was at the beach early one morning, jogging along the shore, when a carload of young men drove by. With their torsos hanging out of the windows, they shouted in unison, "Go for it, baby!"

That day, I decided to celebrate!

I was dating Albert, who had declared when we first met that he intended to marry me and that he was planning to "court the hell out of me" in the meantime. That's what he did for a year and a half. He also was supportive of everything I wanted to do.

I decided to design, promote, and present a workshop for women my age, calling it, "Celebrate You!" and Albert suggested that I call the newspaper and ask them to run an article about the workshop. When I did not get a response from the editor, I called a reporter whose writing I had seen and asked to meet with her. We sat in a booth at the Nighthawk Restaurant as I told her a little of my life story.

She said she would like to write a story about me personally, mentioning the workshop, but would have to consult her editor. She called back two days later to say that she had the go-ahead, and she came to my home for another interview. She brought a photographer, who took some flattering pictures, one of which appeared in the paper.

On Wednesday, August 24, the day of my 50th birthday, there it was, on the front page of the "Life" section—a large, flattering picture with the article. Here is what it said:

Take Columbus. "You know," Peggy Grose says from the booth of a quiet Austin restaurant, "the world used to be flat."

It is a statement. She fixes dark eyes and waits for the response. "You know why?" she challenges. She holds the beat, one-two-three. "Because everybody *said* it was flat."

What Peggy Grose feels that it has to do with herself and other women of her age can be summed in one concept: self-perception.

Not all those perceptions are positive. "I'm not as pretty as I used to be because I have some wrinkles," she says. "Men won't notice me because I'm 50." Her voice quickens. "My ideas are not as good as other people's. If I make a mistake, that's the most important thing about me that day. If I fail, that is awful."

The point is made.

She goes back to the stubborn explorer. "Columbus went against all the thoughts of his world," she says. "Even his crew was hostile. I can imagine people on the shore were saying,"—she raises her voice, mimics 15th-century Spaniards screaming from the sand—"'Come back, you fool! You're headed for disaster!'"

Peggy Grose leans back. The man in a booth behind her turns around curiously.

Today, as she turns 50, she is a Dale Carnegie Course instructor and sales representative and a consultant for the National Corrective Training Institute for certain felony and misdemeanor offenders. Her plan for tomorrow includes owning a company—where she will serve as a communication counselor in office, family, and personal relationships—and directing a self-exploration workshop for women her age.

During the workshop, women will jot down a list of self-concepts, which are put in a paper bag. The point of the exercise is that there's more than one way to look at things. The point of the workshop, simplified, is to look at and, if necessary, challenge the concepts of their lives.

The philosophy of Peggy Grose is simple: People can control their lives. She casually mentions EST training, a Zen concept, and an exercise of envisioning yourself in a desired situation. Which is not to say she is a throwback to the '60s, a believer in quick answers and simplistic explanations. She takes what she needs and leaves the rest. "It's part of my growth," she says. "It's contributed to but doesn't run my life."

And that, says Bob Setty, psychologist and regional coordinator of the National Corrective Training Institute, is the mark of a good counselor. "They are not tied to one sort of system that they have to push everybody into. A good therapist works well with everything," Setty says.

Here the reporter told the story of the rose bush, which I told earlier in this memoir, adding:

It would not do. By the time she left Kerrville after three years, Peggy Grose had bloomed. She directed summer camp, conducted employee interpersonal relationship training for several businesses, became an instructor for Parent Effectiveness Training, and wrote a column for the newspaper on family harmony.

Peggy Grose is the daughter of antebellum Georgia, a fourth-place winner of the Miss Georgia pageant, graduate of a Christian college, former encyclopedia saleswoman ("a hard way to make a living"), holder of a master's degree in personal communication from the University of Texas, civil rights worker, mother of four, wife for 24 years, divorced woman for five.

The slow change from spouse to single woman may have begun when the family moved to Kerrville as she was working on her master's degree. "Moving to Kerrville for me was like falling into a deep, dark hole," she says, her eyes appearing to glitter at the memory. "There was no place for me. I didn't want to play tennis in the morning and bridge in the afternoon."

The article continued with the story of my fear of snakes in the outhouse, ending:

"Since then, I've decided that courage is not the absence of fear; it's doing what you have to do, knowing what probably will be waiting for you." She never found a snake.

The phone began to ring at 7:00 on the morning the article appeared, and I enrolled 44 women that day.

I also heard from a man who called every time he could get through, with the same proposition, "How would you like a 10-inch d—k?" I hung up each time, but finally said, matter-of-factly, "Hey, look, you're tying up my phone, so don't call anymore." I haven't had a single obscene phone call since that day. I'm not complaining, understand.

I held the workshop twice, once at the Hyatt Regency Hotel and again at Green Pastures, an old home that was converted into a lovely restaurant and surrounded by huge oak trees.

It was an all-day affair with a delicious and colorful luncheon in a quiet setting, for only $50. Governor Ann Richards' secretary attended and gave it high praise. An acquaintance called to say that some of her co-workers at the bank were interested in attending but wanted to know what my credentials were that justified the cost of the event.

I gave it up eventually, because of the expense and effort it took to promote it with only fair attendance, but first I consulted the governor about the problem.

She wrote back, "From the fundraising experience of my own campaign, I discovered that women are not yet comfortable with spending money on themselves or on their causes and interests." And yet, this is exactly what the workshop was about!

The universe will support whatever we believe about ourselves, whether it's positive or negative.

CHAPTER SEVENTEEN

DETACHMENT

It felt strange that, by the time I visited my parents the first weekend of October, they had made no comment about the article I had sent. I arrived there on Thursday night for a family reunion and was leaving Savannah on Monday afternoon to return to Texas. As we sat down for lunch on Monday, I questioned, "Well, I assume that y'all didn't like the article for some reason, as you haven't said a word about it."

I was dumbfounded at Mama's vitriolic response. She told me how hurt she was by the comment in the article that I had to go to the outhouse alone. She thought it was a bad reflection on her as a mother and said some awful things to me that day. Again, she thought it was all about her and that it was all negative. She was devastated that I had sent copies to all the relatives.

Daddy was a little embarrassed that I mentioned the outhouse, but he was not hurtful. He later wrote to me, saying how sorry he was that she attacked me so. "I can't believe your mama said those things to you," he added.

It had been a huge honor and triumph for me, getting my picture in the *American-Statesman* in Austin, the capital of the state of Texas, with that wonderful write-up. Mama utterly trashed it. It seemed as if she had spent years cultivating this beautiful flower; then proceeded to beat it to death.

On that day, I declared my independence from her and vowed that from that day forward, I would never again look to her for any approval or appreciation of any kind. I owed her much but had to stop paying with my soul.

I slowly realized that her abusiveness came from nothing more than her fear of not being loved. It was not about me at all. I could detach at that point. I saw my lifelong pattern, one of striving for approval and appreciation and, in the face of none, trying harder.

The metaphor that came to mind was this: Let's say that, for years, I had been going to the Giant Food grocery store looking for chocolate chip ice cream only to learn, time after time, that they had none. Yet, I kept going back to the same store and, time after time, leaving empty-handed. Finally, realizing that they simply had no chocolate chip ice cream, never had had it, and never would have it, I began looking for it in a different place. I had learned my lesson.

When she learned that Daddy had been diagnosed with cancer, Mama took to her bed and never got up again while Daddy continued to putter around the farm until the last few days of his life. On two different occasions, I took leave from my work to go and help, cooking their meals, taking Daddy to the doctor, and cleaning out years of dirt and trash. I waited on Mama, helped her bathe, served her meals in her room, and helped her onto her potty chair.

When she became rude and abusive, I simply said, "Shh. That's hurtful, Mama. I'm here to help you, so you can try to be nice."

She pretended to faint, clutching her chest and gasping, "Oh, you've hurt me so. Now you've spoiled our visit."

I'm happy to say that at this point, she didn't get to me and that on the day she died and on the day of her funeral, I shed not a tear. The only thing I felt sad about was that I wasn't sad.

One is supposed to feel sadness when one's mother dies, for heaven's sake. On the other hand, isn't it sad that as much as she wanted to tie me to her in every way, she managed to destroy any chance of our having a healthy, close relationship as mother and daughter.

***Letting go does not mean giving up,
and it doesn't mean you no longer care.***

18

CHAPTER EIGHTEEN

FINDING MY HANDSOME PRINCE

I kissed quite a few frogs during my "singlehood," before I found my handsome prince. Among the frogs I did not kiss was the professor who brought me his résumé and the guy who brought coupons to help pay for dinner—when he figured out the balance on the bill, he informed me of my share.

And there was the man I met through a personals ad. (What was I thinking?!) During lunch, when I asked him how old his children were, he replied, "Oh, they's growed!"

Oh, and there was the newly divorced man who said he wanted to spend time with me so that I could help him with his problems. A small Voice whispered, "Run for your life!"

Then there was the rather well-known writer who proposed on our first encounter. Without asking anything about myself, he announced, "I don't need a date; I need a wife. I need an attractive wife who can pick up and go with me on trips and attend social occasions at the last minute, so you'll have to do something about that fifteen-year-old boy of yours. And I'll let you know right now that I don't pick up my beer cans or empty my own ash tray. And, by the way, what are you doing about your weight? You're a little wide in the hips". In addition, he brought his own six-pack, all of which he consumed before I sent him on his way.

I had a different experience one day at a speaker's luncheon when an attractive man kept smiling at me from across the room, much to my delight. After the meal and the presentation, here he came, smiling broadly. As he neared me, however, his face fell as he exclaimed, "Sue! Oh…you're not Sue."

I met Jim 20 years ago, when a friend inadvertently put us together. I say "inadvertently" because she liked him herself, and I lost a good friend over it. I was looking for a job, and she gave me the number for Jim Kilpatrick, a car salesman who she thought might help me get a job selling cars. I liked his voice on the phone because it was pleasant and had good energy, but I didn't know whether he was married or single.

I put on my best suit and high heels that Thursday morning and walked into one end of the long showroom. The first man I saw was not very attractive, and I thought, *I hope that's not Jim.* No, it wasn't, but he led me down the length of the room to where Jim was. Along the way, I saw some other men that I hoped were not him. Finally, as we approached a tall, handsome fellow, I thought, *I hope that's him.* And sure enough, my escort called his name, "Jim? There's someone here to see you."

Jim invited me to breakfast at Jack in the Box, where he assured me that I didn't want to sell cars at their place, but asked if he could call me.

I said yes.

We both knew immediately, with a quiet kind of knowing, that we would be together for good and were married on the first day of May, 1988. Jim wanted to go right down to the J.P.'s office, but I insisted on having a wedding with my family and friends present. We were married in a city park by Rev. Rainbow Johnson, a good friend, and her husband Freddie sang a solo *a cappella*, except for the peacocks. This park had been a private residence before being donated to the city and with the house came a couple of these birds. As Freddie reached a high note, one of the peacocks joined in the song, much to the amusement of all.

I made my dress from the pink silk sari with Malayan silver embroidery that I had brought from Singapore and Jim, his son Kyle, my sons Mark, Paul, Daniel, and Justus were all dressed in white summer tuxedoes with pink cummerbunds.

Celebration!

I tease Jim sometimes, asking him, "Do you realize that I used to be married to a Ph.D., and now I'm married to a car salesman?"

He just smiles knowingly. Jim is partially retired now but still working for the same company in a different capacity. Jim may have been a car salesman, but he was also a social worker, helping people find a car they could afford and one that would serve them well. If a customer showed interest in a car that he had doubts about, he would tell them so. He often drove a customer to the highway department to get a driver's license or made their first insurance payment. He often helped a homeless person who came into the store asking for a handout or gave him a ride to the bus station. His customers loved him.

A story that typifies Jim is about a man who wandered into the dealership on one of those cold, wet days that we occasionally have in Austin in winter. He was dressed in a flimsy jacket that was not nearly adequate for such a day, and he was obviously "not all there." He had hitchhiked from Waco and came in on the pretext of shopping for a car, which was obviously not the case. Jim extracted a number for some relatives in town, but they didn't want to have anything to do with him. He reached the man's mother in Waco, finally, and she instructed them to "send him home."

Jim knew that if he put the man out on the road, he would freeze to death. So he and another softhearted salesman put their heads together and arrived at a solution—the Salvation Army, where they took him for a hot meal and warm bed. Jim has sung the Army's praises ever since.

There is another story that we both laugh about. I had reminded him several times to fix the upstairs toilet that was running slightly, with a low hum. He decided to fix it one afternoon and went to the hardware store for the required kit. It went on so easily and was so effective and Jim was feeling so successful about it that he decided to return to the store to get an identical part to replace the one downstairs.

When he returned home and saw the cat lapping up water running out of the front door, he asked himself, *Is that from the freeze? No, the freeze was two weeks ago.* It was coming from the upstairs toilet. The plug on the tank that Jim had installed had come loose, and the water was leaking through the air conditioning duct into the office below and into the living-dining area. After he stopped the flood, he called me at work, pleading, "Honey, please don't divorce me! I've ruined the house!"

I couldn't come immediately, so he was cleaning up by the time I arrived home. At Toastmasters later, I gave a talk, "My Husband, the Plumber." And any time that he overdoes the teasing in front of company, I threaten to tell this story.

I also like to tease him about the time when we decided to purchase some firewood. He answered an ad in the paper, and before the truck got there, he advised me, "Now you let me handle this. We're going to get just a little bit of wood because when we move into the new place, we don't want to have a big pile of wood to have to take with us. And we're not going to pay the first price he quotes either. *Just leave everything to me.*"

When the man arrived with a whole pickup truck load of wood and Jim saw the wife and those three kids in the truck, he said without hesitation, "Why don't we take the whole thing? It's Christmas Eve, and this man needs the money." We bought about $100 worth of fire wood for the asking price of $165 but made a little family really happy. And Jim, too.

Perhaps the best story of all is about the time that Jim read a report in John Kelso's column in the *Austin American-Statesman.* It was about an Afro-American man in East Austin who had purchased 2,000 worms off the internet for $110, planning to resell them for profit. A neighbor complained, though, and the City informed him in a letter that the sign for the stand was illegal and that he would have to remove it or pay a fine of $2,000. With Kelso's help, Jim found the man and bought the worms from him for $110, leaving the worms with him.

Celebration!

Jim has been a kind and generous dad for my son Dan, who has his own lawn and tree service, works like a slave, but does not manage well. Jim's the one whom Daniel calls when he needs help getting out of some jam—and he often *is* in a jam. Daniel moved in with us one November and stayed for an entire year, sleeping on the sofa and running up our food and utility bills. Jim was wonderful about it, with never a complaint, treating him as if he were his own child, helping him out of many difficult situations, and giving him helpful advice. That's not to say that he doesn't sometimes become thoroughly exasperated with Daniel. We both do.

Why did I marry this car salesman?

Because I could see that this man had the capacity to love me for myself and not what he needed me for. He does not allow me to be co-dependent and is not jealous or needy.

He is enthusiastic about me and about life in general, is passionate about sports, reading, and golf, is a fool about his cats, and cares about political issues, but doesn't have an agenda. He gets a huge kick out of small things—feeding and watching the birds and squirrels, puttering around the house, and cleaning his golf balls. He doesn't hold on to resentments. He has several buddies with whom he works and plays golf and with whom he carries on—and my, how they do carry on! He works hard but knows how to loaf, watches far too much television, never, ever, ever, ever puts anything back where he got it, and is not much into self-improvement. He eats all the wrong things and occasionally runs his mouth when I wish he would cool it. If he finds that someone doesn't particularly like him, he doesn't worry about it. He says, "To heck with them," unlike me. Shucks, I want to be liked and invited over for supper. Jim is still struggling to shed that stifling albatross of fundamentalist religion under which he grew up.

With a heart as wide as the waters, Jim can't pass up a beggar on the street and is well known for the many cheery and chatty notes he writes to people, with humorous drawings. He is extremely bright and articulate, with a quick wit and sense of humor, and makes me laugh a lot.

He weeps over a beautiful piece of music, poetry, or a touching story and makes up risqué songs in the shower, complete with correct rhyme and meter. He often leaves love notes in my shoes or on my windshield, and sometimes drives to my workplace to leave a love note on my steering wheel. He brings me dark chocolate.

We play Scrabble® compulsively.

> **Sometimes, we have to wait a while**
> **to find the thing the soul wants most.**

CHAPTER NINETEEN

FLOYD AND DOVEY

Floyd and Dovey Huff came into our lives when Floyd bought a brand new Subaru station wagon from Jim around about 1994. Floyd was 88, and Dovey was 87; they were a devoted couple who had no children. They frequented garage sales every weekend, so the wagon was perfect for hauling home all their loot.

Floyd had considerable difficulty with such technology as changing the clock in the car twice a year and setting the stations on the radio and went to the dealership and had Jim do it. In fact, it seemed that he found any excuse to stop by.

Floyd was still alert and energetic in the early days of their relationship and a little cranky sometimes. He always put up an argument about the price of the car. Half-jokingly, he complained, "Why, this is highway robbery!" or "It's a holdup!" But he would go away happy, and he and Jim became good friends.

Floyd and Dovey furnished their home and their wardrobes from garage sales. Everything Floyd wore—hats, shoes, pants, ties, shirts—came from others' garages and front yards. They had a closet containing nothing but pants, one full of shirts, and a huge rack of ties. He would stop by the car dealership and challenge Jim, "How much do you think I paid for this Stetson hat?" or "How much do you think these shoes cost me?"

Jim always guessed high in order to make Floyd happy.

Floyd worked over 40 years with the state health department and then was a court bailiff for 20 years or so. As he reached his 90s, his eyesight began to fail so that he really should not have been driving for a long time before he actually quit. Dovey had never driven at all. Floyd quit his job as court bailiff after Dovey fell and broke her hip and he needed to be home to look after her.

He drove his car into an intersection a short time later and was hit by a delivery truck, injuring both of them severely. They both recovered, but Floyd never got over having to give up his license, a trauma that he often talked about with me. Now they were stranded at home with no way to get around without the help of others.

A nephew and his family lived in a rural community outside of Austin, but due to the distance from town, it was hard for them to look in on the elderly pair very often. They took care of Floyd's finances, which were rather complicated; and Dovey's sister who lived nearby did their laundry for them and drove them to the grocery store.

But it was Jim whom they called if they needed a ride to the doctor, to the bank, or to pay a bill somewhere. I went with Dovey to have all her teeth pulled and replaced by dentures, staying with her all day and into the evening and driving her for follow-up visits. By this time, Jim, Floyd, and Dovey had started a ritual that called for Jim to bring Donuts to their house every Thursday morning, Jim's day off. When he arrived with the donuts, he knew the coffee would be ready. I was seldom able to join them on Thursdays because of my work schedule.

Because of his increasingly poor eyesight, Floyd also called Jim if he needed help filling out some document or reading and understanding a notice he had received in the mail. They were having more and more difficulty taking care of themselves and their spacious house, and the time came when they had to face reality and give up their home and many of their cherished pos-sessions. The house sold within a few days, and they had to get out quickly and let go of many items they later wished they had kept. It was a heart-rending experience for them and sad for us to watch as they moved into an assisted-living facility.

It was at this point that I became more involved with those two dear people on a regular basis. Jim and I visited them at their new facility, usually on Sundays. We arrived more often than not while they were eating their noon meal and visited with them and their tablemates and with those at nearby tables. I cut up Floyd's food for him and fed him when his eyesight failed.

We eventually began seeing them three or four times weekly, taking turns in order to spread it out; and we all looked forward to it. I tried to avoid having a certain day or time to visit so that if I couldn't make it for some reason, they wouldn't be disappointed.

They had some way of knowing when we were going to show up, though. When I arrived one Thursday afternoon, for instance, Dovey remarked, "I told Floyd, 'Peggy will probably come this afternoon.'" If I didn't show up when they expected me, they would be very disappointed and say so.

The staff of the facility sometimes called me to help out in some way, even though I always reminded them that I was not a relative. Floyd was nearly blind now and nearly deaf, too, and Dovey was in a wheelchair. She was his eyes and ears, and he was her legs.

Dovey fell and hurt her head after about a year at the assisted living home, an injury she never got over. I rushed to the emergency room as soon as I heard about it and witnessed one distraught husband. I stayed until Dovey was settled in her room and Floyd snug in a lounge chair beside her bed. He never left her side for 24 hours.

A friend came the next day for Floyd who needed food, a bath (badly), and some sleep. That evening, Dovey asked me to bathe her face with a warm cloth and I got a pan of warm water and gave her a sponge bath while she purred. She was so thin and fragile that it was like bathing a tiny bird. I wept, overcome by the joy of being able to do this for her.

She would never return to their assisted-living apartment. Floyd had been showing some signs of dementia, and when Dovey went to the hospital, he was moved to "The Harbor" in the same facility, for those in various stages of mental decline. Jim began going every other day to shave him, an intimate thing to do, and they developed an even stronger affection for each other.

Floyd was so anxious to see Dovey that we finally agreed to drive him to visit her at the rehabilitation hospital in the northern part of town, to which she had been moved. Along the way, he marveled at all the changes that had taken place since he had been out of his neighborhood and seemed to be thoroughly enjoying himself.

When we arrived at Dovey's room, however, she was not responsive and did not acknowledge Floyd. He held her hand and, laying his head on the bed, wept and pleaded, "Sweetheart, don't you know me? I'm Floyd, your husband. Please talk to me."

It was heartbreaking.

As Floyd's mind deteriorated, he began to think I was his wife, and on one occasion, he pursued another resident and even crawled into bed with her. She didn't seem to mind, however. By the time Dovey was moved to a nursing home nearer us, she was more mentally alert and begged me to bring Floyd. But I knew he wouldn't recognize her, and that it would be devastating for her. I never told her why I didn't bring him, and I think she was still angry about it when she died. The relatives finally did bring Floyd, though, and sure enough, he didn't know her. I heard that she took it pretty hard.

Floyd sometimes expressed his concern that he would die and leave Dovey alone, and I always replied, "Don't worry. You'll be waiting on the other side, and she'll be there before long." When Dovey expressed the same concern, I responded, "Don't worry. He will be waiting for you on the other side, and we'll all take care of you until you are ready to join him." That's exactly what happened.

Floyd died in the summer of 2003 at the age of 97, and Dovey in the fall at age 96. When Dovey died, their picture appeared in the obit column and under it, the caption read, "Together again."

Jim was honored to be asked to be a pallbearer for both services.

We visited their graves last summer at the country cemetery next to the church of Dovey's childhood. What a blessing they were to us.

Giving and receiving are the same,
and they happen simultaneously.

AFTERWORD

This is my story so far, and this is what I have learned.

I have come to realize that I had a part in creating the nature and quality of all of my relationships. I have seen that I lived in my adulthood what I learned in childhood until I learned an alternative way of living.

In childhood, I learned that my worth was based upon how good I looked, how hard I worked, and that I counted—just *not very much.* My lifelong pattern was to over-invest and over-do for others and, in the face of little or no appreciation or approval, to try harder.

I've observed that there are givers and takers in the world and that they always find each other.

I have learned that people will usually treat us in whatever way we allow them to because we shape and reshape others' behaviors toward us by our own behavior and expectations. In other words, we train others in how to treat us.

I finally caught on to the fact that, for some people, there is power in acting weak and helpless and that they avoid being depended upon by making a mess of anything they are asked to do. I learned that one sure way of perpetuating such a person's weakness is by coming to the rescue, doing things that a person can and should do for himself or herself.

I have realized that one certain way to perpetuate another's failures is to rescue him from the consequences of his behaviors and that a sure way of impeding his emotional maturity is to save him from pain. I now see that trying to make someone else "adequate" is demeaning to that person.

I know that trying to live the dreams that someone else has for us is a tragic mistake.

Celebration!

Along the way, I found that a certain path to resentment and self-pity is to over-invest, over-commit, and overdo, expecting commensurate appreciation and gratitude, and that one way out of resentment and self-pity is to realize that much of what I did was my own choice.

In addition, I came to realize that when a person speaks and behaves badly, it's because of wanting to be loved and of being afraid of not being loved.

In the past several years, I have surrounded myself with people, especially women, who care about me, my work, and my well-being. With loving concern, they share my losses and disappointments and celebrate my successes without feeling diminished or threatened themselves.

No blame is intended toward those mentioned in these stories. They surely experienced the stories differently and, perhaps, should write their own. What has happened is no one's fault, and we each can take responsibility for our part.

At this point, I believe I can truthfully say that I have learned that I can do almost anything I need to do for my own or someone else's good. I can talk to almost anybody about anything—drunks, felons, pimps on the street, parents who have lost a child, or old women who have lost their husbands. I can ingest any food or medicine, no matter how vile tasting, if it's for my health and go any place where I must. I have learned to wait for gratification and satisfaction and count my adversities as blessings. They made me who I am and gave me compassion, the ability to endure, and the courage to take a risk.

My goal in writing the book was to tell my experience while entertaining the reader with the stories of my wild and crazy life. For the first time in many years, I feel a sense of peace, with little resentment, fewer regrets, and a lot of gratitude for what Life has laid at my doorstep.

My ex-husband has survived cancer, which appears to have made him a kinder person; and, having married a woman who is not co-dependent, he is less dependent. I made amends to him long ago in a letter, acknowledging my part in the unhappiness in our marriage. I have welcomed him and his wife into my home several times.

Thank you for sharing my story. I hope that reading it has been half as great a blessing for you as writing it has been for me.

At age 74,
I may not be the most gorgeous flower in the garden,
but I am most certainly not a dried up rose bush.

ABOUT THE AUTHOR

Peggy Grose describes herself as affectionate, a people person, an adventurer, a baby freak, a chocoholic, and a good listener. She says that she has always been afraid that she'll miss something, that she tends to "want it all," and that she wants those around her to "have it all," too.

She likes homemaking and decorating, entertaining company, cooking, dancing, swimming, camping, playing Scrabble® with her husband, writing, storytelling, and traveling afar. She reads and studies a lot.

Peggy is a licensed therapist, the mother of four sons, and the grandmother of three grandsons and one granddaughter. She is a seasoned speaker, an experienced counselor, a teacher, a group facilitator, and a workshop presenter. She has had considerable training and experience in sales.

Peggy is the author of the popular book *Love and Lemon Pie, Recipes for the Body and the Soul*, a collection of recipes that she has been collecting and using for 50 years and on which she raised her four sons. The *recipes for the soul* are suggestions for communicating in loving and nurturing ways. These are her own thoughts about the two ways we show love—serving food and speaking to each other in loving and respectful ways. She says, "Otherwise, we're just feeding their faces!" The book is in its fourth printing.

She works in an outpatient, drug rehabilitation program and lives in Austin, Texas, with her husband, Jim Kilpatrick, who brings her dark chocolate.

QUESTIONNAIRE FOR DISCUSSION

The following questionnaire is provided in order to assist women, individually or in small groups, in examining the nature and quality of their lives and to encourage growth and greater confidence in their own worth. Enjoy!

What were the subtle and not-so-subtle lessons that you were taught as a child about yourself?

What did you understand about the importance of your existence?

What were some of the admonitions that your parents told you?

Did you feel loved just because you were you or for what someone needed you for?

Or did you believe that your main importance was to please and be a credit to your parents? Did they try to live out their hopes and missed dreams through you?

What dysfunctional role, if any, did you play in your family of origin—hero, lost child, scapegoat, or family mascot?

In what way have you lived that childhood belief and behavior in your adulthood?

What has been the cost of that behavior?

What cultural lies about women have you bought into?

Celebration!

In what way have you contributed to the quality of your relationships- satisfactory or dissatisfactory--by your own behavior?

-by rescuing and doing for another person the things that he can and should do for himself?

-by saving another from the painful consequences of her own behavior and, by doing so, impeding his growth?

-and by too much sacrifice, to your own detriment?

In what way do you, or have you lived someone else's dream for you?

On a scale of 1 through 10, how difficult is it for you to say "no" to an unreasonable request?

What is the result of saying "yes" when you wish you had said, "no" to an unreasonable request?

On a scale of 1 to 10, how difficult is it for you to ask for what you want and need?

Who told you that it was not okay to ask for what you want and need?

What is the result of not asking for what you want and need?

On a scale of 1 to 10, how difficult is it for you to confront someone who has been unfair or hurtful?

Who told you that, if you can't say something "nice," not to say anything at all?

What do you tell yourself about yourself?

Who are the people that you need and are willing to forgive?

What do you need to forgive yourself for?

What in your life do you want to keep?

What in your life do you want to change?

Knowing that, about the only way to change another person is to change ourselves and our own behavior, what can you change about your own behavior in order to change the nature of your relationships?

Close your eyes and imagine yourself as a rose bush. Share this image with the group.

What do you have going for you that you haven't realized to its fullest?

What thoughts and assumptions are holding you back?

What is it that you still want from life?

If you knew that you could not fail, what would you attempt?

Think of the most difficult, painful situation or occurrence that you experienced and from which you learned courage, endurance and transcendence. Share that with the group.

Look at how far you've come.

Write a description of yourself in the future.

What about yourself and your life can you celebrate?

Celebration!

St. Theresa's Prayer

May there be peace within today. May you trust God that you are exactly where you are meant to be. May you not forget the infinite possibilities that are born of faith. May you use these gifts that you have received and pass on the love that has been given you. May you be content knowing you are a child of God. Let this presence settle into your bones, and allow your soul the freedom to sing, dance, praise and love. God's presence is there for each and every one of us.